THE CHRIST, PSYCHOTHERAPY & MAGIC

A Christian Appreciation of Occultism

ANTHONY DUNCAN

SKYLIGHT PRESS

Published in Great Britain in 2012 by Skylight Press,
210 Brooklyn Road, Cheltenham, Glos GL51 8EA

First published in Great Britain in 1969 by George Allen & Unwin, London.

Designed and typeset by Rebsie Fairholm
Publisher: Daniel Staniforth

Cover painting: Christ mocked, painted c.1822, from the reredos screen in
St Paul's church at Parkend, Gloucestershire.

www.skylightpress.co.uk

Printed and bound in Great Britain by Lightning Source, Milton Keynes
Typeset in Adobe Caslon Pro. Titles set in Yana, a font by Laura Worthington.

British Library Cataloguing in Publication Data.
A catalogue record for this book is available from the British Library.

ISBN 978-1-908011-51-0

Contents

Author's Preface

WHY does a Christian parish priest find it worth his while to write a book on a little-known, often bizarre system of speculation like the occult? What has it to do with Christian theology? Who wants to know about it – other than the eccentric and the sinister? How can it possibly have anything to do with the pastoral ministry? Why, in other words, was this book written?

This book is, in part at least, a small act of reparation for a lost pastoral opportunity. A soul for whom Christ died did not receive the help and guidance appropriate to his condition because the writer was in total ignorance of the subject-matter of this book. This ignorance was shared, it may be confidently asserted, with fully nine-tenths of the writer's clerical brethren.

The motive having been supplied, a study of the subject proved at once fascinating and appalling; there seemed no end to it. But Chesterton's maxim, 'If a thing is worth doing, it is worth doing badly,' was the final spur. There is, in fact, no doubt at all that a book about occultism is almost bound to be done badly in that the subject is vast. It is not too much to say that the whole of pre-Christian religious speculation is bound up with it. It is necessary, therefore, to severely limit the scope of any book on the subject, and the concern of this book is a comparatively narrow one, the occult tradition that has become centred on the Qabalah.

We shall be studying what Qabalists describe as the Western Mystery Tradition. I am quite persuaded that the long tradition of Mithraism which Father Hugh Ross Williamson traces in his fascinating book *The Arrow and the Sword*, and which is by no means dead even today, is closely bound up with the Western Mystery Tradition, as was the half-forgotten magico-religious system of the Celts, traces of which are still to be found by those who know where to look. But bounds must be drawn and firmly adhered to. We shall be concerned with the Qabalah as Gentile occultists have received it from the traditions of Judaism.

The Christian and the occultist approach religion from different viewpoints. The Christian is concerned with creeds. 'What do they believe?' the Christian asks. To the orthodox Christian, right belief conditions everything; a man will act in accordance with his convictions.

Truth is paramount; truth about God, truth about man, truth about the relationship between Creator and creation; these are the fundamentals. The occultist, however, is pragmatic and empirical. Experience and results are what he seeks; the whole structure of theology is built up from experience and validated for him by experience.

This book is therefore written from the viewpoint of one who is primarily concerned with beliefs and only then with practices. The Christian reader will find himself asking the question, 'Why do they trouble themselves with all this complexity?' for occult theology is exceedingly complex. The answers are probably twofold. Firstly, the very complexity has about it a considerable fascination; secondly, and more importantly, the system 'works' to the satisfaction of the occultist and it is therefore self-justifying and, to him, self-authenticating.

What are we going to be studying in this book? Fundamentally, the Qabalah is a development of the creation myth about which Judaism has speculated to a much greater extent than most Christians realize. The first volume of Jean Daniélou's *History of Early Christian Doctrine* (concerned with the theology of Jewish Christianity) will supply us with a vast background of speculations which will show the Qabalah to have a venerable, if not always reputable ancestry.

The speculation is man's; therefore the 'coming down' of man from God in creation (or manifestation as occultists would have it, and this is *not* the same thing) is accompanied by a complementary speculation as to man's 'going back' to God. The one thing lacking is Revelation, therefore the whole system is purely speculative and remains so. God is so unknowable, so unimaginable, so 'far away' that the developed speculative system has always pushed God out of sight and posited an ever-growing number of intermediate powers. The one thing desired by a speculator is certainty, and so salvation has been sought by 'knowledge'. Gnosticism and Judaism were very frequently intermingled, indeed Gnosticism has always derived inspiration from Judaism but has tended to lose the strong monotheism of the Jew and introduce instead elements of world rejection on the one hand and pantheism on the other.

In the tradition that we shall study, God is right out of sight, and the occultist, whose great work is the exaltation of himself to the power infinity, thus 'becoming God' (or realizing the Godhead inherent in himself), attains his end by magic; by the acquisition of power.

Let it be said at once that magic does not mean black magic. The occultists whose works we shall study are, by intention, practitioners of 'white magic', and the 'left-hand path' is as abhorrent to them as to the Christian. The Christian may well ask himself if there is in fact a valid distinction that can be made between 'Black' and 'White' Magic; 'Are they not both just magic?' he will say. No answer will be given to this question; the intention of the occultist must be respected if a useful and objective study is to be made. The intention of the present writer is to remain as open-minded as possible, to avoid judgements where possible, and to keep the book as 'open ended' as possible. There will be times when he may seem to have strayed into a theological madhouse, but the journey is worth while.

The book is in three parts. The first consists of three essays which will seek to establish the origins from which the Qabalistic tradition has sprung. These will discuss Gnosis and Gnosticism, the Qabalah in Judaism, and the relationship between magic and mysticism. My debt, in this part, to the scholars Sydney Spencer and G. G. Scholem is considerable, and will be very obvious to those who are acquainted with their excellent books *Mysticism in World Religion* and *Major Trends in Jewish Mysticism* respectively. I ask pardon of Hebrew scholars for my inconsistent rendering of Hebrew words; but Scholem uses one tradition of spelling and the Qabalists another. I have tried to substitute the latter for the former where possible, and in some places I have given both.

The second section contains an examination of the Qabalah as it is found in the modern occult tradition. Here too my debt to other writers is considerable, and I have sought to let the occultists speak for themselves as far as possible, and have quoted at length from a number of authorities, chiefly Dion Fortune and Gareth Knight. An appendix follows this section.

The third and last section deals with the practical applications of Qabalistic occultism; its meditational techniques and their affinities with modern psychotherapy. The relationship between occult meditation and Christian prayer is examined and a short study is made of ceremonial magic and clairvoyance. Appendices follow this section.

I am deeply indebted to Gareth Knight, whose two-volume work *A Practical Guide to Qabalistic Symbolism* is extensively referred to in this book, for his very generous help in making available a great deal of material for study, and also to Dom Robert Petitpierre OSB for his careful criticism of the manuscript. I am indebted, too, to Miss Kathleen Raine for drawing my attention to the *Mosaicall Philosophy* of Robert Fludd which is a very important work enshrining the original conception and purpose of the Christian Qabalists of a former generation in taking over the 'Tree of Life' idea from contemporary Judaism. Unlike the sources quoted in this work, who identify the Christ with the Sephirah Tiphareth, Fludd sees our Lord as the tree itself, as the son or logos in whom the father is made manifest. The Sephirah Kether is, in his words, 'the fountain and root of infinity'. Unhappily I discovered Fludd too late to incorporate him into this study, but the relevant chapters of his work would be read very profitably by a student seeking further enlightenment.

Kyrie eleison

St Paul's Vicarage, Parkend, Gloucestershire
May 28, 1968

PART ONE

THREE
INTRODUCTORY
ESSAYS

Gnosis and Gnosticism

'BE on your guard,' wrote St Paul to the Christians at Colossae, 'do not let your minds be captured by hollow and delusive speculations, based on traditions of man-made teaching and centred on the elemental spirits of the world and not on Christ.' (Col. ii. 8) He is concerned about the shadowy beginnings of a great error which was to come close to stifling the infant Church during the course of the following century and a half. 'You are not to be disqualified,' he continued, 'by the decisions of people who go in for self-mortification and angel-worship.' (Col. ii. 18) Such people, he goes on to say, have lost their grip on reality, for all their apparent wisdom and piety.

It is as well to begin our study with this warning ringing in our ears because exactly the dangers to which the holy apostle was referring will dog our footsteps throughout this work. Indeed it is probably only the present generation of Christians who have found the equipment necessary to submit the whole field of occultism to examination in the light of Christ with any real prospect of uncovering the very real merits and profound insights hidden therein. But before we proceed with this examination, it will be necessary for us to undertake a brief research into the whole field of Gnosticism, for this is undoubtedly a Gnostic philosophy.

The Greek word 'gnosis' means 'knowledge'. It is akin to the Latin 'cognoscere' and to the English 'I know'. A Gnostic, therefore, is one who 'has knowledge'. By the same token, an Agnostic is one 'without knowledge'. The words as they stand are straightforward, but in the context of theology, the word 'Gnostic' has come to refer to one who knows, or claims to know, not the sort of knowledge sought by philosophy or science, but 'hidden meanings' and 'secret doctrines'. Victor White, in his book, *God and the Unconscious,* makes the distinction between 'Gnosis' and 'Gnosticism'. He believes it necessary 'to introduce a distinction between Gnosis and a Gnostic on the one hand, and Gnosticism and what we may call a Gnosticist on the other. By the latter I would understand one who, in addition to being a Gnostic, makes an "ism" of his gnosis.[1] And this knowledge which has been made into an "ism" is what we shall be dealing with in some measure in this work.

Gnosticism, in its classical form, was a product of the Hellenistic age, and this was itself the product in some large measure of the Golden Age of Greek philosophy. In a sense, the passing of the philosophers meant a descent into darkness. The love of reason, the optimism about the universe and its order, and the search for clarity gave place to a delving into mystification for its own sake. There emerged a distrust of reason and a dreadful sense of disorder and chaos. In a sense this represented a natural swing of the pendulum, but there was, allied to this quest for mystery, a contempt for the human body and indeed for physical manifestation at all. White suggests that:

'the philosophers themselves had perhaps contributed much to their own undoing. Already, in that "Golden Age" itself, sceptics were undermining their basic postulates, and the wandering sophists were making it their business to arouse distrust for the senses and for reason among the populace. The charge of "atheism" brought against Socrates was not altogether misplaced. Rational thought demanded the existence of God indeed; but the inferentially established God of Aristotle precisely discredited the gods of the myths and cults, and at the same time failed utterly to fulfil the psychological and social functions which they had met. The established religions themselves – the cult of the gods of Olympus, begotten in a much more primitive and less individualized culture – had become increasingly an exteriorized and perfunctory performance, a social ritual which seemed to intensify rather than satisfy the individual's sense of loneliness, frustration and guilt, to increase his conflicts and need for personal liberation.' [2]

It was the stifling effect of over-much human cleverness which led men away from reason altogether. It was, as we have already remarked, a natural swing of the human pendulum, just as eighteenth-century rationalism provoked a wild and immoderate reaction into romanticism. Each needs the other to keep the balance. The descent into myths, home-grown and imported, was in many ways a necessary advance. There is wisdom in a remark by the founder of the modern quasireligion called theosophy, Madame Blavatsky. She wrote in one of her works, 'The mind is slayer of the real'. But she followed up this remark by constructing a vast mind-system.

The emergence of Gnosticism may be traced back to the 'mysteries' which flourished alongside the popular cults of ancient Greece. Popular religion was very much 'established' and was the affair of the masses. But alongside the exoteric was the esoteric. Mystery cults, very much hidden and private, were practised by small groups of devotees who sought deeper meanings and profounder experience. Among a considerable number, we can perhaps single out two as being of outstanding importance; these are the Eleusinian Mysteries and the Dionysian Mysteries. Sydney Spencer, in his book *Mysticism in World Religion*, has this to say about the first named:

'The Eleusinian Mysteries find their centre in the enactment of the myth of Demeter, the Earth-goddess, and her daughter, Kore, the Corn-maiden, who was identified with Persephone – in her origin a pre-Hellenistic mistress of the realm of the dead ... The myth tells how Persephone, while gathering flowers in the meadows, was seized by Hades, the lord of the dead, and carried off to his kingdom, and how Demeter in her sorrow wandered through the world in quest of her, till at last she was brought back by Hermes at the behest of Zeus. Since she has tasted the food of Hades, Persephone must spend a third of the year with him, but year by year she comes back from the underworld in the spring.'

The fertility-rite origins of this myth are obvious. Spencer continues,

'The ceremonies with which the festival were celebrated were open to all Greeks, and later to men and women of all nationalities seeking initiation. They were preceded by a preliminary process of ritual purification and a lengthy period of fasting – in imitation of Demeter – intended to wash away the stains of the former life of the initiates. Eventually the initiates were led in procession from Athens to Eleusis, where they bathed in the sea and roamed along the shore with lighted torches, thus sharing in the wanderings of Demeter in her search for Persephone. They entered into fellowship with the goddess in their separation and suffering, believing that they would share her triumph over death and so attain a blessed immortality – in striking contrast to the traditional belief of the Greeks that at death men entered a land of darkness and shades. It is sometimes held that the rites were followed by a second drama characterized by a sacred marriage, in which Persephone was wedded to Zeus, and the birth of a holy child – typifying the union of the initiates with the deity and their rebirth to a new and higher life. The final stage of the initiation is known as the *epopteia* or "beholding". The door of the shrine at Eleusis was opened, and the priest of the Mysteries revealed to the gaze of the initiates a sacred object in a blaze of light.'[3]

This sacred object may have been an ear of corn, an epiphany of Persephone herself (the corn-goddess) and a symbol of the initiate's rebirth. There is little mystical content in the Eleusinian mysteries, and yet they may have brought men to a sense of higher things than life or death; sometimes perhaps the initiate's 'vision was no mere looking on. It was a sublimation to a higher existence, a transformation of his being.' [4]

In the Dionysian Mysteries, there was a sense of actual possession by, and union with, the god. Spencer tells us that, 'Dionysus, known also as Bacchus, was a god of vegetation and especially of the vine, and of animal life generally; he was also the lord of the souls of the dead ... The cult spread throughout Greece and the adjoining islands. Its distinguishing feature was its orgiastic character. It was celebrated by a sacred dance, held at night by torchlight; wine was drunk as a sacrament. The dancers felt themselves to be possessed by the god, and through the ecstatic consciousness of divine possession each one was regarded as a personification of Dionysus (or Bacchus); They were called Bacci or Bacchae. Being thus exalted to the plane of the divine, the devotees were sometimes held to attain miraculous powers – powers of prophesy, of the healing of disease, even of controlling the forces of nature.' [5] Dionysus was a dying and rising god. He was the child of Zeus and Persephone. Destined to be the ruler of the world, he was devoured by the Titans who, for their impiety, were destroyed by thunderbolts, the human race springing from their ashes. This is the cause of human imperfection, the evil element of which is purged out by initiation into the Dionysian Mysteries. Dionysus was miraculously reborn, the son of a Phrygian earth-goddess, and the object of the mystery-cult was union with the god who was dead and reborn.

The Orphics, a band of devotees and the first itinerant preachers in Europe, arrived at a doctrine of transmigration of souls, deliverance from which is sought by initiation into the Dionysian Mysteries. (An interesting parallel, in time as well as in thought, with their near-contemporary, Buddha.) As we shall see, the idea of transmigration has survived and is a strong feature of the occultism that this work is concerned with.

The two Mysteries that we have briefly surveyed were joined by others originating in Egypt and in other parts of the Near East. The common feature of them all was the initiation of individuals into a sacred mystery. The desired end was rebirth, or enlightenment, or even 'deification'. In its ceremonial aspect, the mystery was a kind of sacramental drama, or perhaps a form of 'sympathetic magic' in reverse. The essential aim was the inner experience of the initiates, gained through participation in the drama. The climate of religion was profoundly syncretistic, but it was also vaguely monotheistic. Each god was perceived as an aspect of the one God, and there was no disloyalty implied by initiation into half a dozen different Mysteries. Sometimes the cults were very close to one another.

They were flourishing at the time of Christ and continued in being for two or three centuries thereafter. The whole 'time-bracket' of Hellenistic Mystery is some eight hundred years.

Perhaps the most striking of the mystery-cults was that attached to Mithras, a Persian god of light, whose cult was widespread in the Roman army and thus was to be found throughout the Empire. Spencer describes the cult as follows:

> 'The myth related how Mithras slew a wild bull (the first creation of the supreme god, Ahura-Mazda), from whose blood sprang the rest of living nature. The central rite in Mithraic temples was thus the ritual slaughter of a bull. There was also a sacrament of bread and water mixed with wine, the wine being said to spring from the blood of the bull. The sacrament celebrated the last meal Mithras took, along with Helios, the sun-god, and other companions. From the bread and wine initiates gained the power to conquer evil spirits; they were also penetrated by a divine substance which gave them the assurance of immortality.'[6]

The Mithraic Mystery was confined to men (a unique feature) and was marked by a strongly ethical approach to life. There were seven grades of initiates, corresponding to the seven 'heavens' of popular contemporary theology, and Mithras was the helper of the soul by whose grace the soul returned to the heavenly light.

The Great Mother cult, originally a fertility rite, initiated the devotee into union with a god who died and was reborn to a higher state. Attis, consort of the goddess, was unfaithful to her and, in remorse, castrated himself and died. The goddess however, restored him to life and made him immortal. At his festival, in the spring, the devotees identified themselves with his tragedy to the extent of lacerating themselves in their frenzy. A feature of this mystery was the 'taurobolium' in which a bull was sacrificed on a grid over a pit in which lay an initiate. His drenching in the blood of the slaughtered bull was understood as being, in some sense, a cleansing from sin. The myth of Isis and Osiris, an Egyptian cult, had similarities with the Great Mother cult, and there were many others.

In the light of modern psychology, especially that of the school of Jung, we are able to recognize, in all these cults, the expression of many of the fundamental archetypal symbols. The enlightenments, the secret knowledge obtained for the initiate by the sacramental dramas of initiation, came from those hidden depths known to us as the Collective Unconscious. Thus recognized for what they are, they are not to be despised for they were real enough although less 'transcendental' than was perhaps supposed. There was nothing supernatural about these cults, nothing in the truest sense mystical. The Western Mystery Tradition, which we shall be dealing with in this work, seeks to obtain for its initiates 'knowledge' from the self-same depths. It is by no means impossible that genuine mystical experience may have accompanied certain of these rites, and this will have depended upon the underlying intention of the initiate. What was he seeking? Did he seek God or the things of God? In all religious endeavour this is the fundamental question. *It marks the point of divergence of mysticism and magic.*

In the course of any written study of such a subject as Gnosticism it is necessary to take matters in succession whereas in fact they overlapped considerably. There was a considerable overlap of the mystery cults that we have described with the immediate forerunner of Gnosticism as it is usually understood. This immediate forerunner was the Hermetic movement which owed its name and inspiration to a legendary sage of ancient Egypt called Hermes Trismegistus (Thrice-greatest Hermes), deified after his death as the god Thoth (father of Osiris) and identified with the Greek god Hermes. There is much confusion and interchange between pantheons and their myths, but this troubled the ancients little. The teachings attributed to Hermes appear to date back to the first two or three centuries AD. There is little knowledge of Hermetic communities, but such as there were seem to have been esoteric brotherhoods, operating a Hindu-like system of master and pupil, such as later distinguished the later alchemists. Their philosophy was broadly Platonic in its later developments and there is evidence of Jewish influence. Unlike the mystery cults which were really magical in character, the Hermetists seem to have been genuinely mystical in their approach. 'It is through mystical experience that man attains liberation. In that experience, at its greatest intensity, the soul is wholly absorbed in the vision of God … In the ecstatic vision of the divine, man's being is deified; he passes into the divine Light.' [7] The Hermetic mystics saw the divine grace as being embodied in ten 'powers' or 'rays'. These are described as divine knowledge, joy, temperance, justice, truth, etc. The whole, taken together, give somewhat the same picture of the divine personality as St Paul's similar teaching as to the 'fruit of the Spirit' (Gal v. 22). There is no sign of Christian influence in the Hermetic movement, but in the movement which we must now investigate, it is considerable. The final product of the Hellenistic age was the movement known to theologians as Gnosticism.

In a sense, all that we have described hitherto may be generally described as Gnosticism. In all this, there has been a search for *Gnosis* on the part of the initiates – 'knowledge', 'understanding', 'enlightenment'.

The search has been in part mystical, in part magical. A large part of the quest has been for the revelation of secrets. Gnosticism properly so called, however, seeks a knowledge which is somewhat different. But it will be helpful if, first of all, we outline the general scheme of beliefs which Gnostics held in common. Once again, Spencer's admirable treatise will help us.

'There was a considerable variety of Gnostic sects in the first three centuries of the Christian era, but they borrowed their writings from one another quite freely. It was common ground among them that the physical world was not a divine creation, but the outcome of a pre-mundane fall – the fall of the Demiurge into matter, or the fall of Sophia or another of the numerous aeons (powers emanated from the supreme God) with whom the Gnostics peopled the invisible world. In man – or rather in certain men, since the Gnostics in general limited the divine principle to a few – there was a spark of divinity, and it was their aim to secure its release from the sphere of matter, *to which it was bound by the chain of rebirth* [my italics] and its return to the higher realm from which it came. As in contemporary Judaism, the soul was believed to pass through the spheres of the planets in its ascent to the celestial world. The spirits which ruled these spheres were conceived as hostile to man. In order to overcome their resistance, it was necessary to know their names. To win salvation, it was necessary also to know the nature of the soul and the secrets of the higher worlds. *"Not baptism alone sets us free,"* said a Gnostic writer, *"but Gnosis* – who we were, what we have become, where we were, whither we have sunk, whither we hasten, whence we are redeemed, what is birth and what rebirth"* [my italics again]. The myths which provide this information tell in some instances of a Redeemer whose help is needed to bring man deliverance. In the Christianized Gnosis of the second and third centuries, which was the object of attack from the Church Fathers, the Redeemer is identified with Christ.'[8]

Built in to the whole structure of Gnosticism is the idea of an aristocracy of those who are 'in the know' as opposed to the masses who are not. This is expressive of a deeply rooted human instinct. The Gnostics – or perhaps they are better described as Gnosticists – divided mankind into 'haves' and 'have nots' on a spiritual plane. There were those in whom the divine spark might be found and who, by initiation and *Gnosis*, might be rescued from their evil material environment; and there were the 'masses' who are in any event doomed to perish. The distinction is between spiritual people and fleshly people. Occasionally a third category is met with, the 'psychic'. The function of Christ, as the Gnosticists chose to understand him, was to bring 'secret knowledge' in his capacity as the emissary of the supreme God, to enable the 'spiritual' people to return to the light.

The neo-Christian Gnosticists were what theology calls 'Docetists' to a man. Docetism represents a tendency in the early Church to consider the sufferings, indeed the humanity, of Christ as apparent rather than real. St Paul, in his letter to the Colossians, warned against these 'hollow and delusive speculations' and 'traditions of man-made teaching'. The author of the Johannine Epistles is also concerned with this problem: 'Do not trust any and every spirit, my friends; test the spirits, to see whether they are from God, for among those who have gone out into the world there are many prophets falsely inspired. This is how we may recognize the Spirit of God: every spirit which acknowledges that Jesus Christ has come in the flesh is from God, and every spirit which does not thus acknowledge Jesus is not from God' (1 Jn. iv. 1-3). These early Christian Docetists are described bluntly as antichrist, both in the passage quoted and also in the second Epistle (2 Jn. 7). The docetic tendency reached its peak in the second century among certain Gnosticists who claimed that Christ miraculously escaped the ignominy of death by 'casting his likeness' on either Judas Iscariot or Simon of Cyrene. It is this latter-day Docetism which has found its way into the Islamic Koran.

Victor White observes that, 'it is customary, and certainly valid, to distinguish Gnosticism by certain common characteristics of belief, certain common patterns and features of the myths, certain common practices, which will be found in greater or less degree among all or most of these gnosticist sects. First and foremost among these, though perhaps more often assumed than openly declared, is the primary, the supreme, value attributed to Gnosis itself. Most authorities will agree with Professor Legge to define gnosticism as "the belief that man's place in the next world is determined by the knowledge of it that he acquires in this". At least tacitly underlying all truly gnostic writings is the assumption of the possibility of liberation, not by faith, love or deeds, but primarily, even solely, by knowledge – knowledge of that kind of introverted intuition which we have seen gnosis to be, and understanding "intuition" with Jung as "perception by way of the unconscious".' [9]

The writer goes on to underline the twofold dualism of which we have already become aware; a dualism in mankind as between 'spiritual' and 'fleshly', and also the dualism on the cosmic scale between the world of spirit, which is 'good' and the world of matter which is 'bad'.

For the bulk of our knowledge of the Gnosticists themselves, and of their teachings, we are obliged to look to the great advocates of the orthodox faith who confronted them. These, Irenaeus, Bishop of Lyons

(c. 180); Hippolytus, Bishop of Rome (c. 230); and Epiphanius, Bishop of Salamis (c. 375) were remarkably fair and objective in describing an error which they abhorred. The fathers pointed to Simon Magus, who appears in Acts (Ch. viii), as one of the first Gnosticists. In his own opinion (according to Justin and Irenaeus) he had come down from heaven to redeem his followers by imparting to them 'knowledge'. His mission was to those who are capable of being redeemed – the 'spiritual' people. The Dead Sea Scrolls, productive of a vast literature already, reveal that the Essenes were a Jewish Sect who were peculiarly subject to external influences, among them, Zoroastrianism. There is much 'chariot-mysticism' (which we shall meet in the next essay) and a good deal of apocalyptic writing. The discovery, in 1945, of forty-four Gnosticist treatises at Nag Hammadi in Egypt, serves to underline the Jewish background to a great deal of Gnosticism.

The Nag Hammadi documents consist of a number of books ascribed to various Old and New Testament characters, purporting to give 'secret doctrines' to eager Gnosticist readers. There are teachings ascribed to Hermes and also to Zoroaster. There are, however, three books called 'gospels' which are most interesting. One, the 'Gospel of Truth', may have been written by a second-century Gnostisict called Valentinus, and appears to be referred to by the fathers in their refutation of the Valentinian Gnosticists. It consists of a series of meditations on the meaning of salvation, as given by Jesus, and also upon the mystical significance of his Holy Name. A similar 'gospel' is attributed to Philip; the third, however, is a collection of our Lord's sayings, some familiar, some unfamiliar, which is called the 'Gospel of Thomas'. It begins with the words: 'These are the secret words which Jesus the Living spoke and which Didymus Judas Thomas wrote. And he said: He who will find the interpretation of these words will not taste death.' Although susceptible of a non-Gnostic interpretation, the 'knowledge-seeking' import of these words is clear. There is much more in this same 'gospel' which is tarred with the same brush. Underlying all the Gnosticist writing we find this dualism, this world-hating, this desperate desire to find an interpretation of the scripture which is more 'spiritual'. Together with this, we find a retreat into magic and false mysticism which issues, in later days, as Quietism and Quakerism with, so often allied to it, a darkening and gloomy world-renunciation, falling through Manichaeanism to its nadir among the Albigenses of the thirteenth century.

'The earliest Christianity, arising as it did out of Judaism, held firmly to the belief that God had acted in the past, was acting in the present, and would continue to act in the future. Some Christians, like some Jews, devised over-precise timetables for God's future action, and when the coming of the end of the world was delayed, they took refuge in dualistic spirituality. Losing the Christian faith in the return of Christ or the Jewish faith in the coming of God's Anointed, they looked only for the escape of the divine spark or true self from the evil world of matter and sin. At this point they became vulnerable to speculations derived from Greek philosophy or Oriental religions. They became vulnerable to Gnosticism. They became Gnostics.' [10]

Gnosticism is a sad business, but it is also a fascinating one. Victor White comments, upon certain of the Gnostic writings: 'an experienced psychologist knows better than to despise even lunatic ravings: he knows that in them he may find an insight into the interior life of the psyche seldom given to the so-called sane and "normal". The very concentration of the gnostic's "libido" [in its Jungian sense of the psychic driving-force or undifferentiated energy] in the activation of the interior images may make of his loss our profit. And many of the Gnostics were certainly no lunatics. In the earlier part of an anonymous Gnostic work called the Pistis Sophia we may witness, besides many of the more unhealthy features I have mentioned, a courageous process of confrontation with the archetypal images which can arouse nothing but amazed and reverent admiration.' [11] White goes on to regret that the contemporary Christian critics of Gnosticism were not better psychologists. Irenaeus, for example, is seeking to be strictly just and fair, but he is a busy diocesan bishop, not a professional psychologist. He is more concerned with *what* the Gnosticists said than *why* they said it.

Gnosticism is currently fashionable. It is staging a come-back. The great psychologist Dr C. G. Jung made numerous references to it in his works. In his book *Modern Man in Search of a Soul* he claims that modern man 'is somehow fascinated by the almost pathological manifestations of the unconscious mind. We must admit the fact, however difficult it is for us to understand, that something which previous ages have discarded should suddenly command our attention. That there is a general interest in these matters is a truth which cannot be denied, their offence to good taste notwithstanding. I am not thinking merely of the interest in the psycho-analysis of Freud, but of the widespread interest in all sorts of psychic phenomena as manifested in the growth of spiritualism, astrology, theosophy and so forth … We can compare it only to the flowering of Gnostic thought in the first and second centuries after Christ. The spiritual currents of the present have, in fact, a deep affinity with Gnosticism … *What is striking about Gnostic systems is that they are based exclusively upon the manifestations of the unconscious* [my italics] and that their moral teachings do not baulk at the shadow-side of life. Even in the form of its European revival, the Hindu Kundalini-Yoga shows this clearly. And as every person informed on the subject of occultism will testify, the statement holds true in this field as well ...

'I do not believe that I am going too far when I say that modern man, in contrast to his nineteenth-century brother, turns his attention to the psyche with very great expectations; and that he does so without reference to any traditional creed, but rather in the Gnostic sense of religious experience. We should be wrong in seeing a mere caricature or masquerade when the movements already mentioned try to give themselves scientific airs; their doing so is rather an indication that they are actually pursuing "science" or knowledge instead of the *faith* which is the essence of Western religions. The modern man abhors dogmatic postulates taken on faith and the religions based upon them. He holds them valid only in so far as their knowledge-content seems to accord with his own experience of the deeps of psychic life.'[12]

What is known to its adherents as the Western Mystery Tradition exactly accords with Jung's description of a Gnostic system – one based upon the manifestations of the unconscious – and essentially seeking 'knowledge' in the best tradition of that ancient Gnosticism of which it is the successor. To say this does not in any way pronounce a value-judgement upon it. What it does do is make clear certain terms of reference, and it also suggests the possibility of certain limitations appearing which must be recognized if justice is to be done to the subject.

References

1   Victor White, OP, *God and the Unconscious*, Fontana, p. 209
2   White, pp. 208-9
3   Sidney Spencer, *Mysticism in World Religion*, Pelican, pp. 128-4
4   W. F. Otto, *The Mysteries*, p. 26
5   Spencer, p. 125
6   Spencer, p. 155
7   Spencer, p. 145
8   Spencer, pp. 149-50
9   White, pp. 209-10
10   R. M. Grant & D. N. Freedman, *The Secret Sayings of Jesus*, Fontana, p. 62
11   White, p. 213
12   C. G. Jung, *Modern Man in Search of a Soul*, pp. 238-9, (quoted by White pp. 203-205)

The Qabalah and Jewish Mysticism

IT would not be too much to say that the whole field of Jewish mysticism is a closed book to the great majority of Christians. Indeed few Christians know, or have made it their business to care, what their Jewish brethren have been doing since the middle of the first century. The dialogue has been limited and inhibited by mutual dislike and mistrust. An evil history has frustrated all efforts at understanding, and these have been few enough in number. The climate is at last changing, and it is now possible for the Christian to take note of what his Jewish brother has been doing in the way of worship and theological speculation; this can only be a profitable exercise for the distinctively Jewish thought-forms were those chosen by the incarnate Life as ideal, and the context of our Lord's whole life on earth was Jewish and Jewish exclusively. It can hardly fail, therefore, that the Christian will find in later Jewish thought much that he will be able to appreciate and value, and relate to his own faith as a Christian.

It will be the task of this essay, therefore, to outline the main course of the development of Jewish mysticism, with especial reference to that great tradition called the Qabalah. It is from this Jewish main stem that that form of occultism known as the Western Mystery Tradition has sprung. Its Gnostic origins have been indicated in the previous essay. This study will seek to complete the background picture. In this essay, however, we shall not be concerned with the uses to which the Qabalah has been put by Gentile occultists in the nineteenth and twentieth centuries. This is the burden of the main part of this work. In this essay, we shall confine ourselves to the strictly Jewish tradition.

The great Jewish scholar G. G. Scholem writes: 'What is to be regarded as the general characteristic of mysticism within the framework of Jewish tradition? *Qabalah, it must be remembered, is not the name of a certain dogma or system,* [my italics] but rather the general term applied to a whole religious movement. This movement, with some of whose stages and tendencies we shall have to acquaint ourselves, has been going on from Talmudic times to the present day; its development has been uninterrupted, though by no means uniform, and often dramatic.' [1]

The movement certainly springs from tendencies which are to be found within the canon of holy scripture, and two general headings come to mind as being the 'roots' from which much later Jewish mysticism has sprung. These are, first, the mystical experiences recorded in the major prophets: the vision of Isaiah in Ch. vi, and that of Ezekiel in Ch. i and elsewhere being the most outstanding. These may perhaps represent the foundations of the later 'throne mysticism' and 'chariot mysticism' with which we shall deal shortly. The second 'general heading' is the whole field of apocalyptic literature, some of which is to be found within the Old Testament (Daniel and 2 Esdras, for example), and a great deal of which is to be found outside the canon of scripture but contemporary with much of it. These two general headings, the visionary and the apocalyptic, are by no means mutually exclusive; on the contrary, they merge.

'The apocalyptic writers are primarily concerned with the revelation of things to come, like the end of the present age and the advent of the Messiah. But they set out also to make known the secrets of the unseen world; and the revelation which they bring is presented as having its basis in a certain experience. That experience is substantially identical with the central feature of the type of mysticism known as Merkabah (chariot) mysticism, which was inspired by the prophetic vision described in Ezekiel i. The Apocalyptic books are ascribed to ancient seers, like Enoch, Abraham, or Baruch, who ascend to Heaven, where they see the divine glory and receive a revelation of things to come. Thus in the Apocalypse of Abraham, written in Palestine towards the end of the first century, Abraham ascends to heaven with the angel Yahoel, his celestial guide. There he sings a song of adoration and ... then sees the divine throne, covered and encircled with fire, and a chariot with fiery wheels. His visionary experience reproduces the main features of Ezekiel's vision, but it is evident that we have here something more than a literary composition.' [2]

Light and fire feature very prominently in the imagery of the Merkabah mystics; Abelson, in his book *Jewish Mysticism*, tells of traditions concerning Rabbi Eliezar who, when expounding the mysteries of the Merkabah to his master, was surrounded by fire from heaven which burnt up all the trees in the field! The same scholar tells of yet another incendiary mystic, Rabbi Jonathan ben Uziel, who was so illuminated by divine fire during his meditations that birds flying above him were, in modern parlance, 'shot down in flames'. [3] The exaggeration is of course the poetry of later enthusiasts who, like all Hebrews, thought in concrete and pictorial terms and not in abstractions. The point is made and taken. The aim of the Merkabah school of mystics was to ascend into Heaven, and indeed in the Hebrew work known as 3 Enoch, a Rabbi called Ishmael is recorded as having done so. Again we must recognize the poetry of those who sought to describe mystical experience, ecstasy and rapture, without the vocabulary to do so. St Paul is more successful in his restraint in 2 Cor. xii. 2-4 (written in Greek) when he says, 'I know a Christian man who fourteen years ago (whether in the body or out of it, I do not know – God knows) was caught up as far as the third heaven. And I know that this same man (whether in the body or out of it, I do not know – God knows) was caught up into paradise, and heard words so secret that human lips may not repeat them.' The saint is describing a profound state of mystical prayer, and a Talmudic tradition tells of four rabbis of the first and second centuries who attained somewhat the same state, or who at any rate were believed to have entered paradise during their earthly life and who were known as the Yorde Merkabah which some have translated as 'riders in the chariot' (God's Throne) but which Scholem prefers to render as 'descenders to the Merkabah'. An odd feature of the language of Merkabah mysticism is the way in which attainment to the mystical degrees is spoken of as 'descent', whereas all the imagery is that of 'ascent'.

There is a considerable literature of which Scholem writes:

'All our material is in the form of brief tracts, or scattered fragments of varying length from what may have been voluminous works; in addition there is a good deal of almost shapeless literary raw material. Much of this literature has not yet been published, and the history of many texts still await clarification. Most of the tracts are called "Hekhaloth books", i.e. descriptions of the "hekhaloth", the heavenly halls or palaces through which the visionary passes and in the seventh and last of which there rises the throne of divine glory.' [4]

There is a distinct connection in thought between this stream of Jewish mysticism and the movement which invaded both Jewish and Christian life known as Gnosticism, the subject of the previous essay. In the Hekhaloth books the ascent of the soul is resisted by hosts of gate-keepers, reminiscent of the Gnostic rulers of the heavenly spheres. 'In order to continue its journey in safety, the soul needs a pass – a magic seal consisting of a secret name – at each new stage of its ascent. *Jewish mysticism is thus intermingled with magic in this phase of its growth.*' [5] [my italics]. But for all the outward resemblance between Gnosticism and Merkabah mysticism, there is a great gulf between them. The idea of

God as King represents the real departure, for to the Jews this idea was paramount and very much so in the Hekhaloth. 'The aspects of God which are really relevant to the religious feeling of the epoch are His majesty and the aura of sublimity and solemnity which surrounds Him.'[6]

There is no idea whatever of the divine immanence. God is worshipped as purely transcendent, and another notable thing is *the almost total absence of love FOR God!* The love of the Jewish mystic for his God is to be found much later in history, not here. There is, as Scholem points out, an almost exaggerated consciousness of God's 'otherness'. There is no idea of mystical union between the soul and God. 'The Creator and His creature remain apart, and nowhere is an attempt made to bridge the Gulf between them or to blur the distinction.'[7]

We may, however, wonder if there is, perhaps, a 'bridge' after all. In 'The Book of the Secrets of Enoch' (2 Enoch) we find Enoch entering the seventh heaven. God commands the archangel Michael to take away 'his earthly robe' and 'clothe him with raiment of my glory'. This having been done: 'I gazed upon myself, and I was like one of His glorious ones, and there was no difference' (Ch. xxii. 8-10, quoted by Spencer). In yet another text, the 3 Enoch referred to earlier, Enoch is identified with the archangel Metatron. The name Metatron is obscure; Scholem considers the odd un-Jewish ending 'tron' to have, perhaps, been a feature of a number of esoteric angelic names in some long-lost 'secret doctrine'. A mediaeval Jewish view of angels, quoted by Abelson, considered that some angels were created while others were divine emanations. This latter seems to be the case as far as Metatron is concerned in the eyes of the Merkabah mystics. He is described as 'Prince of the Presence', 'Prince of the World', and even as the 'Lesser Yahweh'. Metatron, according to Rabbinic tradition, is the angel of whom God said, 'Behold, I send an angel before thee ... My name is in him' (Exod. xxiii. 20 ff). The Name of God is, as Abelson points out, 'a kind of essence of the Deity himself'. Metatron is thus 'a link uniting the human with the divine ... a heavenly co-worker with God'.[8]

The significant fact about all this is that Enoch, in his ascension, is identified with an emanation of God – in other words he is 'deified'. The Jewish mystics of the Merkabah may have shrunk from drawing that conclusion explicitly, but perhaps it may be that the gulf in their minds between creator and creature was a shade less than absolute. The archangel Metatron will be met with again, but here he makes his debut.

Merkabah mysticism, in its later stages, produced a book of great importance, and one which would appear to represent the beginnings of the Qabalah. This book is the *Sepher Yetzirah* or 'Book of Creation', and appears to have been written some time between the third and sixth centuries AD. Frequent references to the first chapter of Ezekiel seem to connect it with the Merkabah school. It is concerned, as its title suggests, with the problem of creation. Scholem considers it to be the earliest extant speculative text in the Hebrew language.

> 'Mystical meditation appears to have been among the sources from which the author drew inspiration ... its chief subject-matters are the elements of the world, which are sought in the ten elementary and primordial numbers – Sephiroth, as the book calls them – and the twenty-two letters of the Hebrew alphabet. These together represent the mysterious forces whose convergence has produced the various combinations observable throughout the whole of creation; they are the "thirty-two secret paths of wisdom", through which God has created all that exists. These Sephiroth are not just ten stages, or representative of ten stages, in their unfolding; the matter is not as simple as that. But "their end is in their beginning and their beginning in their end, as the flame is to the coal – close your mouth lest it speak and your heart lest it think".' [9]

The word 'sephirah' (plural, sephiroth) may be connected with the Hebrew word 'sappir' meaning sapphire, which is used in the description of the throne-chariot of God in Ezekiel i. 26. The book *Sepher Yetzirah* is extremely obscure. It is possible to understand it as meaning that the ten sephiroth emanate out of each other, or out of God. Some scholars consider that the writer identifies the sephiroth directly with the elements of creation – the spirit of God, ether, water, fire, and the six dimensions of space. However they are understood, they represent an entirely new departure in Jewish mystical thought. The sephiroth are said to represent form rather than matter; 'it is the twenty-two letters which are the primal cause of matter. The world of corporeal things arises from the conjunction of the two. The letters, like the sephiroth, are a divine emanation ... It was taught traditionally that the world was made by the word of God: the letter-mysticism of the "Book of Creation" represents in essence simply an elaboration of this conception, the assumption being that Hebrew is a sacred language and so the language of creation.' [10]

The letter-mysticism enshrined in the *Sepher Yetzirah* is most strange to the Gentile mind. However the idea that Hebrew is, as it were, the language of heaven is firmly embedded in the Old Testament, although the text does not betray this fact to the casual reader. When God 'uttered' in creation, when he said 'let it be so', and it was so, the Jew takes it for granted that God 'uttered' in the Hebrew language! This is the key to the tremendous reverence accorded to that language. Hebrew being the language of heaven, no book could claim ultimate authority if it were written in any other tongue. This explains, perhaps, why the beginning and end of Daniel are in Hebrew, whereas the middle is in the popular variant, Aramaic. The Hebrew is necessary to it if it is to carry final authority. At the council at Jamnia in about AD 100, when the rabbis finally defined the canon of scripture, the Greek-language Septuagint versions were rejected and if there ever were any Hebrew versions of Greek-language originals such as the *Wisdom of Solomon*, they were probably destroyed.

There is a connection of which we must take note between the *Sepher Yetzirah* and 'theurgy' or 'spiritual magic-making'. There is much highly ceremonious ritual connected with this period, including 'putting on of the name' in which the magician clothes himself in a garment into which the divine name has been woven. 'The revelation sought through the performance of such rites is identical with that of the Merkabah vision. The "Prince of the Torah" reveals the same mysteries as the voice which speaks from the throne of fire: the secret of heaven and earth, the dimensions of the demiurge, and the secret names the knowledge of which gives power over all things.'[11] Scholem says that the theurgic doctrines form a kind of meeting-place for magic and ecstaticism and that the theurgical element is emphasized in a number of writings, among which is one with the title 'The Magical use of the Psalms'. 'The latter have had a long: if not quite distinguished career in Jewish life and folklore.'[12]

The meeting-place of mysticism and magic will be discussed in the third of these introductory essays, and it is a subject to which we shall return very frequently. The Merkabah mysticism, of which the *Sepher Yetzirah* is a part, did not all degenerate into magic, pure and simple. There was a strong moral element with a good many references to penitence, and the various palaces or stages through which the soul had to pass were related to ascending stages of moral perfection; nevertheless 'the form of. mysticism which it represents takes no particular interest in man as such; its gaze is fixed on God and his aura, the radiant sphere of the Merkabah, to the exclusion of everything else. For the same reason it made no contribution to the development of a new moral idea of the truly pious Jew. All its originality is on the ecstatical side, while the moral aspect is starved, so to speak, of life.'[13]

The great movement within Jewry known as Hasidism is really outside our terms of reference, our main intention in this essay being to discover the origins and development of that system of thought called the Qabalah. Hasidism is another 'ism' within Judaism. Flowering in thirteenth-century Germany, it represents. a restoration of balance and a return to those principles which the non-Jew would more readily recognize as Jewish than the rather extreme and exotic tendencies that we have considered hitherto. Samuel the Hasid (devout), his son Judah and their friend Eleazar of Worms are the leaders of this movement and their writings are to be found in the *Sepher Hasidim* (Book of the Devout). Of the Hasidim, Spencer says:

> 'the essential fact was the cultivation of a mystical piety leading to a constant sense of the divine Presence. Whereas in Merkabah mysticism stress was laid mainly on the training of the visionary and ecstatic faculties, so that the soul might be caught up into the celestial world and perceive the divine glory, among the Hasidim the emphasis was on the living of a life of devotion which found its fulfilment in the vision and love of God.' [14]

The extreme transcendentalism of the Merkabah school is countered by an equally pronounced immanentism among the Hasidim. True to Old Testament tradition, there is no extreme asceticism. The value of married life is emphasized and this is true of Jewish thinking generally. A gentle, somewhat Puritan piety is demanded of a Hasid. He must be forgetful of self and he must be careful of his duties to the community. At its best, mediaeval Hasidism represents a highly developed spirituality, but the element of magic is not absent. The idea of the mysterious power of sacred names is much in evidence; a Hasid in popular legend was believed to possess power over the forces of nature, and in the writings of Eleazar of Worms there are tracts on magic side by side with discourses on the mystical way of life and the nature of God.

We have now arrived at a point at which it is possible to see the tradition known as the Qabalah beginning to take shape and emerge as a tangible philosophy. In the middle of the thirteenth century, while Hasidism was flourishing among the Jewish communities in Germany, the other mainstream of Jewish mystical speculation began a great leap forward in Provence and, later on, in Spain. The personality who might be said to have begun this new movement was one Abraham Abulafia, born at Saragossa in 1240, much travelled throughout the Near East, and who settled and produced much of his literary output in Italy towards the end of the century. The aim of Abulafia, the vocation which he believed had been divinely laid upon him, he summarized as, 'to unseal the soul, to untie the knots which bind it'. Briefly, Abulafia perceived that the human soul is kept within the limits determined by our sensory perceptions and emotions, and because it is full of these, it finds great difficulty in perceiving the existence of spiritual forms. The problem was one of helping the soul to perceive more, *to increase its range of consciousness* without becoming blinded and overwhelmed by the divine Light. Abulafia sought what might be described as an 'absolute object' for meditation; one capable of stimulating the depths of the human soul and freeing it from its enslavement to ordinary perceptions. The 'absolute object' that he discovered was the Hebrew alphabet! For Abulafia, the letters in which the divine language is written are more than mere letters, more than abstract symbols. Abulafia was a Jew. The divine language is the means whereby the word of God is communicated; and not merely the word – the WORD. God *is* his word.

> 'Basing himself upon the abstract and non-corporeal nature of script, he developed a theory of the mystical contemplation of letters and their configuration, as the constituents of God's Name. For this is the real, and if I may say so, the peculiarly Jewish object of mystical contemplation: the Name of God which is something absolute, because it reflects the hidden meaning and totality of existence; the Name through which everything else acquires its meaning and which yet to the human mind has no concrete, particular meaning of its own. In short, Abulafia believes that whoever succeeds *in making this great Name of God, the least concrete and perceptible thing in the world, the object of his meditation, is on the way to true mystical ecstasy.'* [15]

Abulafia was deeply impressed with the *Sepher Yetzirah*; it underwrote all his convictions. He expounded a discipline which he called 'hokhmath ha-Tseruf' (science of the combination of letters) which is a system of permutation and combination of letters. His system, developed in a number of works throughout his life, sounds strange to a non-Jew, but nevertheless it was clearly aimed at inducing in his disciples a capacity for profound contemplation which, it was ever hoped, would issue in ecstasy. He taught a technique of breathing and bodily postures closely akin to yoga, and he held a high opinion of the relationship in spiritual things between master and pupil. The master is not merely a human being, he held, 'he personifies the angel Metatron, a semi-divine principle, or even (as is sometimes said) God Himself. A man is indeed not merely confronted by his master; he is identified with him, and so with Metatron or with God ... In this doctrine of identification with the divine, familiar to us in certain phases of Christian, Islamic and Indian mysticism, Abulafia stands alone among the Jewish mystics.' [16]

Abulafia, the master of prophetic Qabalism, was utterly opposed to the practice of magic. In this he differs from the great majority of Qabalists;

indeed he was unpopular among his contemporaries. He represents the ecstatic movement in Spanish Qabalism, whereas the theosophical movement, which suspects his teaching, has prevailed. About this latter we shall have much to say hereafter. As Scholem points out, the teachings of Abulafia can be put into practice by almost anyone who tries, and the criticism – and virtual suppression – of his work by more orthodox Qabalists may have been moved by a fear of the dangers of uninstructed lay mysticism and its tendency towards heresy. 'Jewish mysticism tried to meet this danger by stipulating in principle that entry into the domain of mystical thought and practice should be reserved to rabbinic scholars. In actual fact, however, there has been no lack of Qabalists who either had no learning whatsoever, or who lacked the proper rabbinic training … The pristine enthusiasm of these early ecstatics frequently lifted the heavy lid of rabbinic scholasticism.' [17]

Some scholars have tried to identify Abulafia as the author of a book which appeared during his lifetime and which presents Qabalistic thought in a very highly developed and systematized form. This book is the *Zohar* (brightness, or splendour). This attribution will not stand investigation, however, as the *Zohar* represents the very antithesis of the doctrines of Abulafia. It is the *Zohar* which gives us the 'Tree of Life' which later occultists have taken and built upon.

It will be useful, however, to make mention of an earlier work, the product of the same school, called the *Bahir* (brightness). This book, described by Scholem as 'highly obscure and awkward', is in part a compilation of several older texts, some related to Merkabah mysticism, and one at least of a decidedly Gnostic character – the *Razar Rabba* or great mystery. This, considered by many to be an important esoteric work, is perhaps the channel by which Gnostic terms, mythologems and thought-forms found their way through to the thirteenth-century school of Spanish Qabalists, to exert a great influence upon the shaping of their theosophy.

But we must return to the *Zohar*. Its author is believed to be Moses de Leon, who died in the year 1305. It is a massive work and, in a way to which we have become accustomed, it takes for granted that, underlying all things is the creative power of speech. The Jewish veneration of the Hebrew language, which we have observed throughout this survey, is unmitigated in the *Zohar*. Language, and in particular the language of the *Torah*, is the key which unlocks the mysteries of existence. It is the link between the 'above' and the 'below' – the Kingdom of Heaven and the Kingdom of Earth.

The central feature of the teaching of the *Zohar* concerns the Sephiroth which we encountered in the *Sepher Yetzirah*. Their numerical significance is swallowed up in a wholly new understanding. They are manifestations of the godhead, degrees of divine manifestation. 'They are at once qualities or attributes and agencies of God – the creative names which God gave Himself. The world of the Sephiroth is the hidden world of divine language which underlies the phenomenal universe. They represent both phases of the hidden life of the godhead and means of his self-revelation to man. They are channels or "flowings forth" (emanations) of the divine light whereby the transcendent God became immanent in the world. They are active in the soul of man – itself an emanation from them – and so they enable man in his turn to play a creative part in the divine order and to unite himself with them.'[18] At once we observe a new clarity of thought emerging in the foggy field of Jewish mysticism; what has hitherto been intangible begins to attain some degree of concretion.

'The hidden God, the innermost Being of Divinity so to speak, has neither qualities nor attributes. This innermost Being the *Zohar* and the Qabalists like to call *"En-Soph"*, i.e. the infinite (without end).'[19] 'His Being is utterly beyond all knowing. In a certain sense He is *"ayin"* (nothing) – the undifferentiated background of being. Yet he may be described as *"Or En Soph"* – the infinite light – and from the unutterable radiance of his light there spring the ten lights of the Sephiroth which illuminate the minds of men. Taken as a whole, the Sephiroth form "the one great Name of God". Yahweh, which is equivalent to the divine presence as it is manifested in the order and harmony of creation.'[20] Scholem makes it plain that the Sephiroth are not to be understood as secondary or intermediate spheres, interposing between God and the universe. They are not 'outside' God; on the contrary, they are 'in' God. It is now time to examine these spheres, the 'Tree of Life', or diagrammatical representation of this understanding of God and the things of God.

For the succession of the ten Sephiroth, the Qabalists have a number of more or less fixed terms which are often employed by the writer of the *Zohar*. More often, however, he employs various symbolic terms. The fixed or common names of the Sephiroth are as follows:

1. Kether Elyon	The Supreme Crown of God; virtually indistinguishable from En-Soph, and yet distinct
2. Hokhmah (Chokmah)	The Wisdom or Primordial Idea of God
3. Binah	The Intelligence of God
4. Hesed (Chesed)	The Love or Mercy of God

5. Gevurah (Geburah), or Din — The Power of God, chiefly manifested as the power of stern judgement and punishment. Sometimes called 'pachad' – fear

6. Rahamim or Tiphareth — The Compassion of God, mediating between Judgement and Mercy. Also – but according to Scholem, rarely – the Beauty of God

7. Netsah (Netzach) — The Lasting Endurance of God

8. Hod — The Majesty of God

9. Yesod — The Basis or Foundation of all active forces in God

10. Malkhuth (Malkuth) — The Kingdom of God, usually described in the *Zohar* as the 'Keneseth Israel', the mystical archetype of Israel's community; or as the 'Shekhinah'

The above, taken from Scholem's rendering (but with the variant spellings in brackets), give us the ten spheres of divine manifestation. They form, together, the 'unified universe' of God's life. They are the 'mystical crowns of the Holy King'. 'He is they and they are he.' They are the ten names most common to God and they form, together, his one great name. They are God's varying aspects, and they are the ten stages of the inner world through which God descends from the innermost recesses down to his revelation in the Shekhinah.

'The ten Sephiroth constitute the mystical Tree of God or tree of divine power, each representing a branch whose common root is unknown and unknowable. But En-Soph is not only the hidden Root of all Roots, it is also the sap of the tree; every branch representing an attribute, exists not by itself but by virtue of En-Soph, the hidden God.'[21] The ten Sephiroth are grouped into three 'triangles' of which we shall hear more later. The contemporary English Qabalist, Gareth Knight, describes them as the 'supernal or archetypal triangle' formed by Kether, Chokmah and Binah; the 'moral or ethical triangle' formed by Chesed, Geburah and Tiphareth; and the' astral or psychological triangle' formed by Netzach, Hod and Yesod. These triangles are those of modern occultism, but the principle is the same. The tenth Sephirah, Malkuth, unites and harmonizes the rest. It

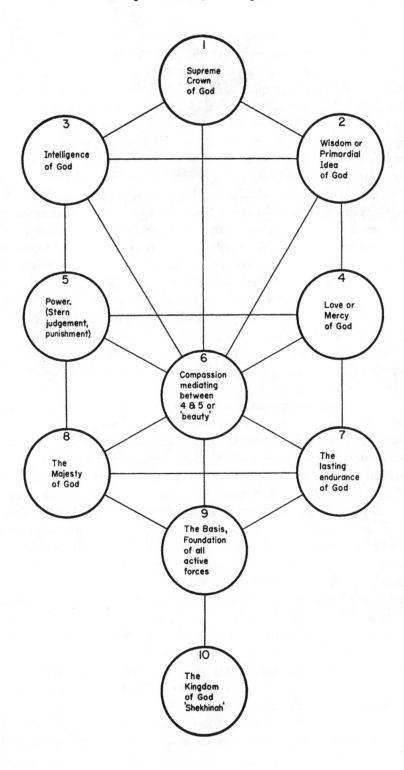

is sometimes called 'the kingdom', sometimes 'the Shekhinah', the presence of God in the universe, including his special manifestation in the lives of men and in hallowed places. 'Among the Hasidim, the Shekhinah is identified with the inner glory of God, whereby he reveals himself to men. As Abelson has shown, the thought of the Shekhinah plays a prominent part in rabbinical literature, where it is often identified with the Holy Spirit. In the *Zohar*, the Shekhinah receives a feminine character. It is described as the Queen, and is conceived alternately as the daughter and the bride of God. The Sephiroth as a whole are said to be the offspring of the union between God and the Shekhinah, which is also regarded as the mother of each individual Israelite. She is the archetype of the community of Israel, and she is at the same time present in the actual community.'[22]

The Qabalistic doctrine of evil and the fall need not concern us here. The Shekhinah is, in a sense, 'exiled' through the fall; she is 'Rachel weeping for her children' and, in the later teachings of Isaac Luria, the exile of the Shekhinah will only end with the coming of the Messiah. The philosophy represented by the *Zohar* has its mystical side. Ecstasy is stressed little, but the idea of attainment of union with the divine is all-important. There is no sexual asceticism whatever; marriage, in true Jewish style, is regarded as a sacred mystery reflecting the union of God with the Shekhinah.

The doctrine of transmigration of souls, already met with in this essay, was regarded as an exceptional destiny, brought about, above all, by offences against procreation. The probable author of the *Zohar*, Moses de Leon, strongly condemned the idea, common in the East, of transmigration into non-human forms of existence. For the later school of Messianic Qabalism, a sixteenth and seventeenth-century development, the doctrine of transmigration is taken to be a fundamental law. Its form is similar to the Hindu, and it finds a kind of mystical expression in the exile of the Shekhinah due to the fall of Adam, and the experience of Jewry in Exile throughout the world. It is perhaps significant that the Qabalistic school which saw in transmigration a fundamental doctrine, and whose leader was Isaac Luria (born 1584), rose out of the expulsion of the Jews from Spain in 1492, and a new sense of desolation which then overcame that unfortunate people as a result. For the school of Luria, the process of restitution (Tikkun) is the purpose of Israel; the restoration of cosmic harmony is her task; that is why she is scattered – in order to 'lift everything up'. The coming of the Messiah will restore all things and end the exile of the Shekhinah.

The despair which underlay the disciples of Luria issued in a sad heresy called Sabbatianism, named after a manic-depressive called

Sabbatai Levi (born 1626) who proclaimed himself Messiah at Gaza in 1665. Promptly arrested by the Turks, he turned Muslim to save his skin. Astonishingly, he was accepted as Messiah by large numbers of Jews, especially in Poland, his apostasy notwithstanding. Feigned apostasy became a brief fad and in reaction from this sorry and disastrous episode a new emergence of Hasidism has flourished from about the beginning of the eighteenth century to the present time.

Hasidism is, however, within the Qabalistic tradition. There is no hard and fast distinction between a Hasid and a Qabalist, the difference is one of approach or emphasis. It is notable, however, that magic, a feature of Jewish spirituality throughout its development, still has its place even in modern Hasidism. The founder of the modern movement, Israel Baal Shem (born 1700) provokes this comment from Scholem:

'Consideration must be given to ... the close connection between mysticism and magic throughout the history of the Hasidic movement. It is as though the personality of Israel Baal Shem had been created solely for the purpose of confusing the modern theorists of mysticism. Here you have a mystic whose authentic utterances permit no doubt as to the mystical nature of his religious experience and whose earlier and later followers have resolutely taken the same path. And yet he is also a true "Baal Shem", that is to say, a master of the great name of God, a master of practical Qabalism, a magician. Unbroken confidence in the power of the Holy Names bridges the gap in his consciousness between the magician's claim to work miracles with his amulet, or through other magical practices, and the mystical enthusiasm which seeks no object but God. At the end of the long history of Jewish mysticism these two tendencies are as closely interwoven as they were in the beginning, and in many of the intermediate stages of its development.'[23]

This is the point at which we shall leave this brief study of the essentially Jewish origins of the Qabalah. The Gentile occultists regard the Qabalah as a magical philosophy and magic, as they define it, is woven fundamentally into it. In the last of these three introductory essays we shall consider the nature of magic, and its relationship to mysticism; both principles apparently fundamental to man's religious instinct, and both featuring prominently later in this work.

References

1 G. G. Scholem, *Major Trends in Jewish Mysticism*, Thames & Hudson, p. 18
2 Spencer, p. 176

3   J. Abelson, *Jewish Mysticism*, pp. 41 ff
4   Scholem, p. 44-5
5   Spencer, p. 178
6   Scholem, p. 55
7   Scholem, p. 56
8   Spencer, p. 179-80
9   Scholem, p. 76
10 Scholem, p. 181
11 Scholem, p. 77-8
12 Scholem, p. 78
13 Scholem, p. 79
14 Spencer, p. 182
15 Scholem, p. 133
16 Spencer, p. 188
17 Scholem, p. 126
18 Spencer, p. 190
19 Scholem, pp. 207-8
20 Spencer, p. 191
21 Scholem, pp. 213-4
22 Spencer, p. 192
23 Scholem, pp. 348-9

Concerning Magic

MAGIC is in disrepute. In the mind of modern man it signifies conjurers at children's parties, witchdoctors in darkest Africa, or the fairies and wizards of popular folklore. If these images are rejected, then magic is associated with the more sinister novels of Dennis Wheatley and 'Black magic' is assumed to cover the whole field. Indeed, modern man thinks of magic, if he thinks of it at all, as something essentially sinister and malign. Books on the subject tend to emphasize the sensational, morbid aspects of magic. An objective, disinterested examination of the subject is hard to find. Unless we approach the subject as objectively and as disinterestedly as possible, however, we shall almost certainly pre-judge it and condemn it out of hand, and this will be unfortunate, for there is more to it than we might suppose, and – providing we become clear about its nature and its limitations – we shall find it a profounder, and possibly healthier subject than we had imagined.

Sir James Frazer, in his monumental study *The Golden Bough*, sees magic as a relic of man's past; an irrational attempt to escape from the unknown, or to influence the uncontrollable. At its best, he sees it as a bogus form of science. He declares, 'If we analyse the principles of thought on which magic is based, they will probably be found to resolve themselves into two: first, that like produces like, or that an effect resembles its cause; and, second, that things which have once been in contact with each other continue to act on each other after the physical contact has been severed. … From the first of these principles, the magician infers that he can produce any effect he desires merely by imitating it: from the second he infers that whatever he does to a material object will affect equally the person with whom the object was once in contact, whether it formed part of his body or not.'[1] These two principles, called homoeopathic and contagious magic respectively, he proceeds to illustrate throughout the great length of his work. His opinion of magic is low: 'Magic is a spurious system of natural law as well as a fallacious guide of conduct; it is a false science as well as an abortive art.'[2] He divides magic into theoretical magic (a pseudo-science) and practical magic (a pseudo-art) and deals with the latter under the two sub-headings of 'sorcery and taboo' (positive and negative). At the end of *The Golden Bough*, magic is discredited and religion fares only slightly better. 'We may illustrate the course which thought has hitherto run by likening it to a web woven of three different threads – the black thread of magic, the red thread of religion, and the white thread of science, if under science we may include those simple truths, drawn from observation of nature, of which men in all ages have possessed a store. Could we then survey the web of thought from the beginning, we should probably perceive it to be at first a chequer of black and white, a patchwork of true and false notions, hardly tinged as yet by the red thread of religion. But carry your eye farther along the fabric and you will remark that, while the black and white chequer still runs through it, there rests on the middle portion of the web, where religion has entered most deeply into its texture, a dark crimson stain, which shades off insensibly into a lighter tint as the white thread of science is woven more and more into the tissue.'[3] He goes on to wonder what the final colour will be.

Frazer's great work, a classic, expresses a widely held view about both magic and religion which has prevailed from the publication of his work in 1922 to the present day. Magic is finished, but yet 'The word "magic" is out of fashion, though its spirit was never more widely diffused than at the present time.' So wrote Evelyn Underhill in 1911, and her judgement was upheld by Dr C. G. Jung a quarter of a century later in a statement which concluded the first of these three essays. In her own great work *Mysticism* she uncovers a whole dimension which does not appear at all in Frazer's study.

'Magic,' Miss Underhill writes, 'as described by its apologists, is found to rest upon three fundamental axioms which can hardly be dismissed as ridiculous by those who listen respectfully to the ever-shifting hypotheses of psychology and physics.

(1) 'The first axiom declares the existence of an imponderable "medium" or "universal agent", which is described as beyond the plane of our normal sensual perceptions yet interpenetrating and binding up the material world. This agent, which is not luminous and has nothing to do with the stars, is known to the occultists by the unfortunate name of "astral light". ... To live in conscious communication with the "astral light" is to live upon the "astral plane", or in the astral world: *to have achieved, that is to say, a new level of consciousness* [my italics]. The education of the occultist is directed towards this end.

(2) 'The second axiom of magic ... also has a curiously modern air: for it postulates simply the limitless power of the disciplined human will ...

The first lesson of the would-be magus is self-mastery ... real "magical initiation" is in essence a form of mental discipline, strengthening and focussing the will. This discipline, like that of the religious life, consists partly in physical austerities and a deliberate divorce from the world, partly in the cultivation of will-power: but largely in a yielding of the mind to the influence of suggestions which have been selected and accumulated in the course of ages because of their power over that imagination which Eliphas Levi calls "the eye of the soul". There is nothing supernatural about it. Like the more arduous, more disinterested self-training of the mystic, it is character-building with an object, conducted upon an heroic scale.

(3) 'The dogmas of the "astral light" or universal agent and the "power of the will" are completed by a third: the doctrine of Analogy, of an implicit correspondence between appearance and reality, the microcosm of man and the macrocosm of the universe, the seen and the unseen worlds. In this, occultism finds the basis of its transcendental speculations. "Quod superius sicut quod inferius" – the first words of that emerald table which was once attributed to Hermes Trismegistus himself – is an axiom which must be agreeable to all Platonists.'[5]

Evelyn Underhill and Sir James Frazer were both scholars of the first rank; they were also very much of their age, and neither were magicians. Since their works were published there have come available tools for a deeper investigation into the subject of magic than either of them possessed. But we must now attend to magic as it were from within.

The brilliant but bizarre occultist Aleister Crowley (1875–1947) defined magic as, 'the science and art of causing changes to occur in conformity with will'. Crowley's scholarship in occult matters is respected by contemporary Qabalists, but his example is abhorred. He seems to represent in his career everything that a sincere occultist ought not to be and ought not to do. Another magician of some distinction, who wrote under the name of Dion Fortune, was at pains to make it clear that she had no connection whatever with Crowley. She altered Crowley's definition of magic significantly by adding two words; according to Dion Fortune, magic is 'the science and art of causing changes in consciousness to occur in conformity with will'. It is this altered definition which is accepted by the authorities which, in the main, will be consulted in this work. We are already a long way from *The Golden Bough*.

Dr Israel Regardie, a magician of some renown among his brethren, maintains that: 'Magic concerns itself in the main with that self-same world as does modern psychology. That is to say, it deals with that sphere of the psyche of which normally we are not conscious but which exerts an enormous influence upon our lives. Magic is a series of psychological techniques so devised as to enable us to probe more deeply into ourselves. To what end? First, that we shall understand ourselves more completely. Apart from the fact that such self-knowledge in itself is desirable, an understanding of the inner nature releases us from unconscious compulsions and motivations and confers a mastery over life. Second, that we may the more fully express that inner self in everyday activities.'[6]

Dr Regardie makes frequent reference to the psychological teachings of Dr C. G. Jung, and it is clear from his writing that the correspondence between the ideas behind many of the obscure, often bizarre terms of the magician on the one hand, and the more precise terminology of the psychologist on the other, is remarkably close. In the monograph quoted here, he sets a precis of Jung's *Analytical Psychology and Weltanschauung* alongside the passage on the 'astral light' by Eliphas Levi already mentioned by Miss Underhill, and concludes: 'I suggest, then, that what the magicians imply by the astral light is identical in the last resort with the collective unconscious of modern psychology.'[7] Magic, he asserts, is a scientific method, a valid technique whose approach to the universe and the meaning of life is legitimate.

Magic, it has been claimed, concerns itself with the same things as modern psychology; but that is not all that is claimed for it. 'Approaching the matter from another point of view, it may be said that magic deals with the same problems as religion. It does not waste its or our valuable time with futile speculations with regard to the existence or nature of God. It affirms dogmatically that there is an omnipresent and eternal life principle – and thereupon, in true scientific fashion, lays down a host of methods for proving it for oneself. How may we know God? Here, as before, there is a well-defined and elaborate technique for dealing with the human consciousness as such *and exalting it to an immediate experience of the universal spirit permeating and sustaining all things* [my italics]. I say advisedly that its technique is well-defined. For the system has an abhorrence of the attitude of those good-natured but muddle-headed thinkers who, refusing to accept their human limitations as they are now, aim too high without dealing with the manifold problems in the way.'[8]

The orthodox Christian would wish to ask many questions about the assertions in this paragraph, but there is quite clearly emerging a basis for serious dialogue between the contemporary magician, as he reveals himself in his writings, and the Christian.

The relationship between magic and mysticism is a close one, but the two paths are quite distinct and must not be confused. Evelyn Underhill has expressed the difference aptly by stating that 'magic wants to get, mysticism wants to give'. This is undoubtedly true, but the Christian would be unwise to decide at once that, on these grounds, magic should be condemned out of hand. What does magic seek to get? The answer is knowledge; understanding. The magician seeks to know. This is true of the scientist, and he is not usually condemned out of hand for it. Some will say that power is the aim of the magician, but a contemporary magical writer, W. E. Butler is clear about his motives, and the motives he expects of his pupils: 'I desire to know, in order to serve – such is the password which admits to arcane knowledge.' [9] As much is required of a doctor of medicine, so let us not be too hasty to pass judgements. It is the matter of intention which, in the last resort, distinguishes a 'white' magician from a 'black'. Of the seeker after power for its own sake, (or his own sake), Crowley claims that he is isolated from the rest of the universe – 'Such a being is gradually disintegrated from lack of nourishment and the slow but certain action of the attraction of the universe, despite his now desperate efforts to insulate and protect himself, and to aggrandize himself by predatory practices. He may indeed prosper for a while, but in the end he must perish.' [10] This, as a description of the state of mortal sin, is wholly admirable. It is all the more sad that there are not wanting among his erstwhile brethren those who consider Crowley's description to have applied perfectly to himself.

Evelyn Underhill, hostile to the idea of magic, admits of the possibility of 'knowing in order to serve', somewhat obliquely, when she writes: 'We may class broadly as magical all forms of self-seeking transcendentalism. It matters little whether the apparatus … be the incantations of the old magicians, the congregational prayer for rain of orthodox Churchmen, or the consciously self-hypnotizing devices of "new thought": whether the end proposed be the evocation of an angel, the power of transcending circumstance, or the healing of disease. The object is always the same: the deliberate exaltation of the will, till it transcends its usual limitations and obtains for the self or groups of selves something which it or they did not previously possess. It is an individualistic and acquisitive science: in all its forms an activity of the intellect, seeking reality for its own purposes, or for those of humanity at large.' [11]

Magic is aptly described as an activity of the intellect. Mysticism, however, is nothing of the kind. Indeed here is a distinction between the two as fundamental as that of 'getting' and 'giving'. The mystic seeks God. The magician seeks the things of God. The magician uses his intellect, the mystic uses his heart. But lest this latter should seem sentimental, the mystic's endeavour is an absolute act of will – the deliberate quest for the total loss of himself in God. The mystic seeks union with God, and his overriding motive is love.

It is axiomatic for the Christian that he must die in order to live. This simple fact of life has to find expression in everything he is and does. If he loves his own life, he is promised that he will lose it. If he tries ever to give it away in love of God, then he is assured that he will be forever found. Mysticism seeks only 'to be'. Magic seeks 'to know'. The Christian knows that, in Christ, he is in direct touch with reality and that the end of the road for him – if he is faithful – is utterly to be with Christ in God. This is within the realm of mysticism, purely and simply, although it by no means follows that every Christian is therefore 'a mystic'. The great mischief perpetrated by practitioners of magic lies in their claim that magic is the pathway to reality. This is a serious confusion of two quite separate principles. It provokes the charge made against occultism of 'perverted spirituality' and it spells ruin to both the mystical way and the magical. The mere transcending of phenomena – the making of changes in consciousness in conformity with will – does not by any stretch of the imagination entail the attainment of the absolute. 'Magic even at its best extends rather than escapes the boundaries of the phenomenal world. It stands, where genuine, for that form of transcendentalism which does abnormal things, but does not lead anywhere: and we are likely to fall victims to some kind of magic the moment that the declaration "I want to know" ousts the declaration "I want to be" from the chief place in our consciousness.'[12]

It is clear, therefore, that, whatever view we hold about magic as such, it is of the first importance that it is distinguished from mysticism; and in this connection it is unfortunate that the words 'mystic' and 'mystical' are applied as loosely as they are, for they are found to refer to that which pertains to magic quite as often as they are used in connection with true mysticism. This essay has sought to introduce the subject of magic and outline its main terms of reference as we shall meet with it in this work. *It has also sought to avoid passing moral judgement upon it.* These three essays provide a general background without which the study of occultism is carried on as it were in a vacuum. This, all too often the case even in the writings of serious occultists, serves only to obscure that which is of real value and highlight the less substantial, often tendentious, and frequently bizarre speculation which so easily disfigures the whole field of study.

References

1 Sir J. G. Frazer, *The Golden Bough*, (abridged edn), Macmillan, p. 14
2 Frazer, p. 15
3 Frazer, p. 933
4 Evelyn Underhill, *Mysticism*, Methuen, p. 154
5 Underhill, p. 156 & ff
6 Israel Regardie, *The Art & Meaning of Magic*, Helios, p. 44
7 Regardie, p. 88
8 Regardie, p. 45
9 W. E. Butler, T*he Magician; His Training & Work*, Aquarian Press, p. 25
10 Aleister Crowley, *Magick in Theory and Practice*, p. 237
11 Underhill, p. 71
12 Underhill, p. 151

PART TWO

THE MAGICAL QABALAH

The Theology of Occultism

ALEISTER Crowley, in his remarkable book *Magick in Theory and Practice* claims that 'There are three main theories of the universe: Dualism, monism and nihilism ... All are reconciled and unified in the theory which we shall now set forth.'[1] Beyond doubt 'the Master Therion' was satisfied with his reconciliation, but it will not help us in the present study, and indeed a glance is sufficient for an informed Christian to see that the initial statement is suspect.

It is no simple matter to get to grips with what might be described as the 'theology' of the occult. The reason for this is that there are no creeds as Christians understand them. Occultism, like Hinduism, is not so much a religion or a system as a 'general heading' under which a huge variety of speculation flourishes, a good deal of it directly contradictory. Of Hinduism it has recently been written, 'the religious beliefs of different schools of Hindu thought vary and their religious practices also differ; there is in it monism, dualism, monotheism, polytheism, pantheism, and indeed Hinduism is a great storehouse of all kinds of religious experiments'[2] That this is true beyond doubt is quite clear to anyone with a knowledge of Hinduism; and it is no less true of occultism.

Western occultism has been very greatly influenced by Hinduism during the last hundred years or so. The two 'isms' are respectively the Western and Eastern versions of the same basic approach. Perhaps the strongest link that has been forged between them has been the Theosophical Society whose founder, Madame H. P. Blavatsky, settled in India in the year 1878. The movement spread to Europe and the United States some few years later. Theosophy itself purports to derive its teachings from Indian sacred writings, and is a curious mixture of pantheism, magic and rationalism. 'Theosophists deny both a personal God and personal immortality ... they regard Christ as purely human and consequently deny the validity of the Christian revelation.'[3] But it is a mistake to identify occultism as a whole with the Theosophical Society, and indeed there have been 'Theosophist bishops' *(Episcopi Vagantes)* and there exist quasi-Christian sects among whom the expression 'esoteric Christianity' may be heard. Let an example be given: 'In the

Guild of the Master Jesus, which is part of my own organization, the Fraternity of the Inner Light, we work the Mass with power because we apply these (magical) principles. When we first started we were offered apostolic succession for our ministrants, but declined it because we felt that it was better to use our knowledge to make the contacts anew on our own account than to receive apostolic succession from a source that was not above suspicion, and experience has justified our choice.'[4] This makes lamentable reading for an orthodox Christian, but the author is as distinguished and respectable in occult circles as can be wished, and a master of 'white' magic. The Hindu-like syncretism is manifest a few sentences earlier in the remark, 'I am not a Catholic, and never shall be, because I would not submit to their discipline, nor do I believe that there is only One Name under heaven whereby men may be saved, much as I respect that Name, *but I know power when I see it, and I respect it* [my italics].'

It is very difficult not to prejudge the whole question of magic, and the temptation will persist to condemn it out of hand, but the temptation must be resisted if a truly objective view is to be arrived at.

But it is time to attempt a study of occult theology, bearing in mind that we are concerned with the Qabalistic stream within occultism; our investigations must therefore be limited to the general terms of theological reference within which it works. There is no precision, but it would not be too much of an inaccuracy to describe the theological framework as a mixture of Platonism and monism, monism having entered through the Hindu back door.

Platonism is, in general terms, the underlying philosophy behind western occultism, although not always recognized for what it is. The Platonic concept of the perfect world of 'forms', of which this world is an imperfect shadow, is one which has permeated the whole of classical philosophy, and which is not by any means absent from Christian theology (many scholars see, in the Fourth Gospel, an appeal to Platonists in their own language). The hermetic axiom already quoted, *'Quod superius sicut quod inferius'* – or simply, 'as above, so below', is pure Platonism and will be met with again and again in Qabalistic speculation. To the Qabalist, the microcosm, man, is an exact replica of the macrocosm, God. This, it is argued, has the support of holy scripture: 'And God created man in his own image, in the image of God created he him' (Gen i. 27). And the imperfection of the 'shadow' world of man is explained by a doctrine of the Fall (expounded by such authorities as Dion Fortune, Gareth Knight, etc.) which relies on different 'mechanics' than the Christian understanding, but arrives at a very similar result.

Monism, the philosophy that has joined Platonism explicitly from Hindu sources (but implicitly present in all magic-working philosophy), seeks to explain all that exists in terms of a single reality. Chesterton confronts his famous 'Father Brown'[5] with the question, 'Do you not realize in your heart, do you not believe behind all your beliefs, that there is but one reality and we are its shadows; and that all things are but aspects of one thing; a centre where men melt into Man and Man into God?' This is the question that monism *must* ask of us. It is a profound one, but Father Brown gives the only answer – No.

A study of the writings of responsible contemporary occultists reveals that the two main trends, the Platonistic and the monistic, tend to be associated with the two main approaches to the Qabalah. The philosophical, speculative and meditative approach – relatively unknown to the outsider – tends towards Platonism; the practical, magical approach – automatically but usually wrongly associated by outsiders with 'black magic' – tends strongly towards monism. *It is of the first importance to realise that in this, as in all religious systems unregulated by formal creeds, the theology is subordinated to the prevailing emphasis.*

Monism is the philosophy to which we must pay most attention. Briefly, it is concerned with eliminating the apparent dualism of the physical and the psychical by postulating a reality transcending these, of which both are modes.[6] 'The Universe and everything in it constitutes God. The universe is a gigantic human organism and man is a tiny image of it, a toy replica of God. Because he is a miniature of the universe, by a process of spiritual expansion a man can mystically extend his own being to cover the entire world and subject it to his will. It is because all things are aspects of the one thing that all things are grist to the magician's mill. The complete man, who has experienced and mastered all things, has vanquished Nature and mounted higher than the heavens. He has reached the centre where man becomes God. The achievement of this is the Great Work, the supreme magical operation, which may take a lifetime or several lifetimes to complete.'[7] This statement, by a witness undoubtedly hostile to the whole subject, is nevertheless only too true as an analysis of the position of such a magician as Crowley. 'Man can make himself God because he has the divine spark within him,'[8] and, 'by "God" I mean the Ideal Identity of a man's inmost nature. "Something ourselves [I erase Arnold's imbecile and guilty 'not'] that makes for righteousness"; righteousness being rightly defined as internal coherence.'[9] Self-realization is the quest of the Monist, be he Hindu Yogi or occult magician, 'The microcosm is an exact image of the Macrocosm; the Great Work is the raising of the whole man in perfect balance to the power of Infinity.'[10]

Crowley was an outstanding example of a monist who has fallen into the trap which is built in to the very nature of the monist philosophy. Man, seeking to wind himself up into heaven, has fallen headlong into the abyss. The sin of Adam is, in monism, 'theologically justified'. Not all monists fall into the trap by any means, but it yawns at the feet of all.

It will be worth our while to examine the occultist's monism as expounded by a more responsible and typical authority than the bizarre Crowley. W. E. Butler, an authority on the magical side of modern Qabalism, writes:

'The philosophy which underlies magic is the philosophy which appears in the Indian *Vedanta* the philosophy of monism. In this philosophy .God and his universe are seen to be one and the same. But this, it will be said, is pantheism pure and simple. It would be if we were so foolish as to regard nature as the whole of God. We do not only hold the idea of His being in and through His Universe, but we also believe He transcends it. *An immanent and transcendent being is the God of the magical philosophers* [my italics]. But both these terms can easily be misunderstood. If by "immanent" we think of "something" behind manifestation as we see it, then we are beginning to use the philosophic counters of Aquinas, "substance" and "accident". Though this is a perfectly valid distinction, the magical philosopher would go further and say that all manifestation exists as an expression of that substantial being, and *because of that* it possesses Reality after its own kind ... It has sometimes been said that the magical doctrines are doctrines of "emanation", and in one sense this is so. But if by this it is thought that they teach that (in all reverence) God emanates the universe from himself as a kind of cosmic spider spinning a web from Himself, then such a conception is entirely foreign to the magical scheme. The magi teach that the whole universe of matter in all its grades, physical and non-physical, is the manifestation of the very essence and substantial Being of the eternal. ... So it is not matter which is unreal, only the appearance it presents to our consciousness, *and as that consciousness is evoked and expanded, so do we begin to see in all things the presence and very being of God* [my italics].' 11

It will be clear on reading – and perhaps re-reading – this, that there has been a marked change in 'atmosphere'. Monism, pure and simple, has undergone some development. A pure immanentism is seeking to cope with the transcendent, and is changing its nature in the process. In another publication, the same writer says of the Qabalist philosophy: 'It is an "emanationist" philosophy. In the last analysis it is very true to say that God "created" all things, but the way in which it was done as set forth by the Qabalah, is different to the ideas of orthodox Judaism which have been taken over into orthodox Christianity. The great objection of Christian theologians to the "emanationist" philosophy is that it tends towards pantheism, *which can be so easily equated with the idea that "God" is simply the totality of nature. The Qabalah, however, does not teach this* [my italics]. Quite rightly it teaches that God is made manifest in nature, and is immanent in it; but it also teaches that all manifestation, on whatever plane of existence, is only one aspect of the eternal being who reigns transcendent over all. In this philosophy there is no hard and fast division made between spirit and matter. Matter is regarded as the "luminous garment of the eternal", indeed as being an expression of the eternal, and therefore all things are holy in their intrinsic nature.'[12]

Butler's position is nearer to Christian orthodoxy than to pure monism, but it is still some distance away. His 'monism' is stretched beyond its limits, it is not big enough for the job in hand; but Butler himself is a minister of a small sect of the type mentioned above, and his monism is nearer to Christian orthodoxy than Crowley's monism. *The theology varies with the interpreter,* as it does in Hinduism! *There is in all modern Qabalist writing, a very profound ignorance clearly apparent concerning the true nature of Christian belief.* It is an interesting exercise to speculate about this flight, in the middle and late nineteenth century, into quasi-Hindu monism. Was it perhaps a reaction away from the naïve and lifeless transcendentalism of popular Protestant devotion? (i.e. 'I am "here", God is "there"') Did the popular piety of the day, inhibited and suspicious of deep spirituality, provoke not only a reaction within the Church but also one away from and out of the Church? Monism is a deeply 'spiritual' philosophy; far more so than the naïve transcendentalism often still mistaken for Christian orthodoxy! Monism appeals to deeper instincts ; instead of the principle 'God and creation are separate', the principle is 'God and creation are one'. Alas, neither the shallow pietist nor the occultist have yet really grasped the true Christian understanding that all things are IN GOD!

We have spent some time thinking of the monist and magical aspects of Qabalistic 'theology'. But we shall mainly be concerned with another aspect altogether, namely the philosophical. It is as well, however, to have at the back of our minds the main source of danger to the Qabalist as we go on to investigate in some detail the speculative philosophy concerning the emanative manifestations of the unknowable, beginning, as we shall, with the problem of 'negative existence'.

References

1   Crowley, *Magick in Theory and Practice*, p. 1
2   K. M. Sen, *Hinduism*, p. S7
3   Oxford Dictionary of the Christian Church
4   Dion Fortune, *The Mystical Qabalah*, p. 244
5   G. K. Chesterton, *The Dagger With Wings*
6   O.D.C.C.
7   Richard Cavendish, *The Black Arts*, p. 6
8   Cavendish, p. 5
9   Crowley, p. 5
10 Crowley, p. 4
11 W. E. Butler, *The Magician, His Training and Work*, pp. 28-9
12 *Helios Course on the Practical Qabalah*, Lesson 10, pp. 2-3

The Veils of Negative Existence

A T the heart of Christian theology we find the teaching of the Cappadocian fathers, and many others, to the effect that, 'if we say "God is", indicating that in him is the fulness of all that we can conceive of as Being, we must complete it by saying also "God is not" to indicate that the fulness of his Being is far beyond anything that we can conceive of as existing (since all the existents we know are limited and circumscribed by their existence). However, we must remember that this tradition of mystical negation always co-exists, in Christianity, with a tradition of symbolic theology in which the positive symbols and analogies of theological teaching are accepted for what they are: true but imperfect approximations which lead us gradually towards that which cannot be properly expressed in human language.'[1]

This tradition of 'knowing' and 'unknowing' is fundamental to the religious experience of man and manifests itself in various ways in virtually every religious system. The Qabalah is no exception; but the relationship between negation and symbolism is different, if not unique. 'The Qabalists ... do not try to explain to the mind that which the mind is not equipped to deal with; they give it a series of symbols to meditate upon, and these enable it to build the stairway of realization step by step and to climb where it cannot fly. The mind can no more grasp transcendent philosophy than the eye can see music. The Tree of Life, as cannot too often be emphasized, is not so much a system as a method; those who formulated it realized the important truth that in order to obtain clarity of vision one must circumscribe the field of vision. Most philosophers founded their systems upon the Absolute; but this is a shifting foundation, for the human mind can neither define nor grasp the absolute. Some others try to use a negation for their foundation, declaring that the absolute is, and must ever be, unknowable. The Qabalists do neither of these things. They content themselves with saying that the *absolute is unknown to the state of consciousness which is normal to human beings* [my italics]. For the purpose of their system, therefore, they draw a veil at a certain point in manifestation, not because there is nothing there, but because the mind, as such, must stop there.'[2]

The writer whose words have been thus quoted defined magic as the art of causing *changes in consciousness* in accordance with will. The Qabalah, in its Jewish origins, is a speculative system; in occult usage it is a magical method in which meditation upon symbols seeks to enlarge the sphere of consciousness, beyond its accustomed limits.

In his personal mystical experience, St John of the Cross knew God as the 'unknown' and taught that the All was attained as 'nothingness'. Words cannot express the inexpressible, and paradox and contradictions abound. The 'unmanifest' – in the Qabalistic expression – cannot be adequately manifested in words.

> 'The Unmanifest is pure existence. We cannot say of it that it is *not*. Although it is not manifest, it *is*. *It* is the source from which all arises. *It* is the only "reality". *It* alone is substance. *It* alone is stable; all else is an appearance and a becoming. Of this unmanifest we can only say *"It is"*. *It* is the verb *"to* be" turned back upon itself. *It* is a state of pure "being", without qualities and without history. All we can say of *it* is that it is not anything that we know, for if we know anything it must be in manifestation for us to know it, and if it is in manifestation, it is not unmanifest. The unmanifest is the great negation; at the same time *it* is the infinite potency which has not occurred.'[3]

The echoes of St John of the Cross in this (impersonal pronoun excepted), and of many other mystics of many other faiths, remind us that the dilemma over expression is universal. The Qabalah tackles the problem symbolically, and it will be helpful to recapitulate a part of the Jewish tradition outlined in the second chapter of this book.

God, the innermost being of divinity so to speak, has neither qualities nor attributes. This innermost being the *Zohar* and the Qabalists like to call *Ain Soph*, that is to say the infinite. His being is utterly beyond all knowing. In a certain sense He is *ain* – nothing – the undifferentiated background of being. Yet he may be described as *Ain Soph Aur* – the infinite light – and from the unutterable radiance of his Light there spring the ten lights of the Sephiroth which illuminate the minds of men. Of these concepts Dion Fortune writes:

> 'These three veils, Ain, negativity; Ain Soph, the limitless; and Ain Soph Aur, the Limitless Light – though we cannot hope to understand them, nevertheless suggest to our minds certain ideas. Negativity implies Being or existence of a nature which we cannot comprehend. We cannot conceive

of a thing which is, and yet is not; therefore we must conceive of a form of being which, according to our concepts of existence, does not exist, and yet, if one may express it so, exists according to its own idea of existence. … But although we say that negative existence is outside the range of our realization, it does not mean that we are outside the range of its influence. If this were so, we could dismiss it as non-existent so far as we are concerned, and our interest in it would be at an end. On the contrary, although we have not direct access to its being, all that we know as existing has its roots in this negative existence, so that, although we cannot know it directly, we have experience of it at one remove.'[4]

The Qabalah offers itself as a 'map' of manifestation, however, and so we must proceed from the unmanifest to the successive stages of manifestation represented by the Sephiroth. An examination of terms is important before we proceed.

'Manifestation' and 'creation' are terms applied to the same basic phenomenon. The choice of term indicates the approach of the chooser. The Qabalist speaks of manifestation; the Christian speaks of creation. The terms are not interchangeable, however. The Christian would say that God manifests himself in creation, but he would immediately proceed to qualify that statement very substantially. The Qabalist, an emanationist, and a monist at heart, says, 'There is no part of me which is not part of the gods.' Man is the microcosm, the 'lesser universe', which is in and part of the Macrocosm, or greater universe. The two approaches are not, however, totally irreconcilable.

Gareth Knight, in the chapter dealing with the problem of the unmanifest and the veils of negative existence, writes, 'In almost all religious creation myths, creation first occurs as the manifestation of light. But the veils of negative existence refer to the pre-dawn period before darkness has fully given birth to light, and in this shadowy area there are many symbols which attempt to give some understanding of the primordial darkness before anything was. All of them, however, are variations upon the circle or sphere, from the serpent with its tail in its mouth to the "rotund urn" of the alchemists. It is the circular figure, the endless line, which best gives the idea of something which is self-contained, without beginning or ending; with no before or after, that is, timeless; with no above or below, without space. Space and time, beginning and ending, come only with the coming of light, or consciousness, and this is not yet present. It is also as shown in the symbol of the cosmic egg, the germ from which all creation arises. It is also a state in which the opposites are united as shown in the Chinese *t'ai chi t'u* sign. It is the perfect beginning because the opposites have not yet flown apart and the perfect ending because the opposites have come together again. It is at the same time the primal germ and the final synthesis of all creation.'[5]

In arriving at manifestation from the unmanifest, we are – to borrow an image from Buddhism – contemplating a circle whose circumference is nowhere and whose centre is everywhere. Gareth Knight bids us meditate upon 'nothingness crystallizing a centre'[6] which is as it were, 'the fount of Creation, the point 'where life wells up from the deeps of the great unmanifest.'[7] The concretion of this centre is our concern, and of this Mathers writes, 'The limitless ocean of negative light does not proceed from a centre for it is centreless, but concentrates a centre, which is the "number ONE" of the manifested Sephiroth; Kether, the Crown, the First Sephirah.'[8]

References

1   Thomas Merton, *Redeeming the Time*, pp. 25-6
2   Dion Fortune, *The Mystical Qabalah*, pp. 29-30
3   Fortune, *The Cosmic Doctrine*
4   Fortune, *The Mystical Qabalah*, pp. 33-4
5   Gareth Knight, *A Practical Guide to Qabalistic Symbolism*, Vol. I, p. 57
6   Knight, Vol. I, p. 64
7   Knight, Vol. I, p. 66
8   MacGregor Mathers, *The Qabalah*

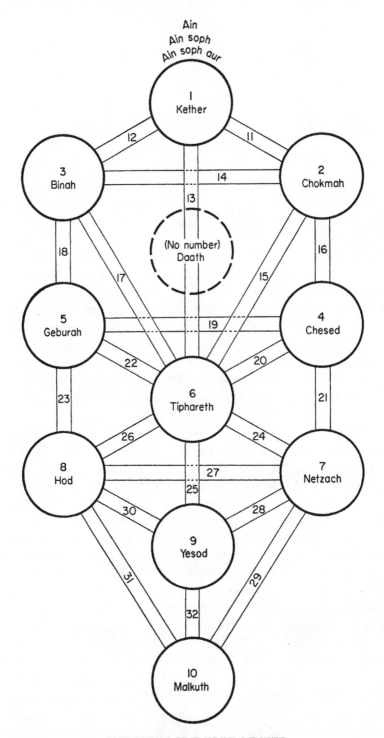

OTZ CHIIM, THE TREE OF LIFE
The Ten Sephiroth (the Objective Qabalah) and the Twenty-Two Paths
(the Subjective Qabalah)

Kether

The first path is called the admirable or hidden intelligence because it is the light giving the power of comprehension of the first principle, which hath no beginning. And it is the primal glory, because no created being can attain to its essence.

THE quotations that will head the chapters that follow in this section are taken from what, to the Qabalists, is known as the *Yetziratic Text*. This writing is first found in Pistorius's collection of Qabalistic writings published in Basle in 1587. The version quoted here (and quoted by both Dion Fortune and Gareth Knight in their works) is a translation made by Dr Wynn Westcott from a publication of the *Sepher Yetzirah* (probably in Latin) by Rittangelius in Amsterdam in 1642, in which this Text appears as a supplement. Of the 'Thirty-Two Paths of Concealed Glory', the first ten 'paths' are the ten Sephiroth of the Tree of Life, and the remaining twenty-two are the 'paths' which connect them.

Kether, in the words of Gareth Knight, is 'manifestation on the point of becoming manifest, the centre crystalized in the midst of non-being, containing within it the potentialities of all to come. It is the supreme height of Godhead although it must not be forgotten that all the Sephiroth are equally holy, being emanations of the one God. Thus Malkuth, the physical world, is as *divine* [my italics] as the highest spiritual sphere, Kether, the crown of creation. Those who consider Malkuth holy without reference to the higher Sephiroth fall into the error of pantheism, which is a half-truth. Those who consider Kether to be holier than the subsequent creation fall into the equal error of denying the unity of God, of setting up a dichotomy between spirit and matter.'[1] The Christian will applaud the healthy rejection of an unreal dichotomy between the 'spiritual' and the 'material' which has so clouded popular Christian thinking so often in history; a key word in Knight's statement, however, is *divine*. Malkuth is as *divine* as Kether. This is not a loose application of words, using 'divine' in place of 'holy'; if it were, then the Christian could, for the moment, rest content with the Tree of Life as it begins to unfold before him, for all creation is 'holy' in that it is God's and rests in God. But the word used is 'divine', and this reflects the occult presupposition that *all things are manifestations of God*. This must be remembered throughout the chapters that follow, although the reader may well wonder why monism and emanationism are *necessary* to the Qabalah. It will occur to many that the whole speculative system would be at least as happy *within* true Christian orthodoxy as outside it. The rebellion of many responsible occult writers is usually against an incomplete or distorted Christian position, and with this the Christian can sympathize.

Knight continues; 'all subsequent creation from the pure force of Kether is a gradual concretion into form of the one divine force. Form is force locked up into patterns of its own making. Force is that which is released when the patterns or forms are broken.'[2] This is somewhat of a key passage, for we shall see as we go on that the unfolding of the Tree of Life is a chart of the progressive expression of force in form. It is a key passage in the understanding of the workings of magic, as we shall discover in due course. The mind of modern man is drawn to such recent manifestations of the principle as nuclear fission.

'To an entity conscious on the lower plane where the form is built,' Knight says, 'the interlocking of the higher forces, causing a form on the lower level, will appear to be a birth. When the form is broken and the forces return to their original higher level the process will appear as a death. To an entity conscious on the higher plane, however, the descent into form of free-moving forces will be considered a death, and the break-up of a form to release the forces will be a birth. In this way it will be seen that birth and death are two sides of the same coin. ... This is the basic pattern of all manifestation and unmanifestation, which we have already seen to be cyclic. It is also the process of the human soul coming down the planes into densest form and subsequently dying to this form and being reborn to the inner worlds, *and then, after a time of assimilation of past experiences in densest form, coming to birth into it again by the death of its freedom of the less dense forms of the higher planes. This is the basic doctrine behind the theory of reincarnation* [my italics].'[3]

Reincarnation, met with increasingly in Jewish Qabalism in chapter two, has become firmly bound up with occult Qabalism in modern times. Without doubt the Hindu influence has been strong here, but it is not clear why a doctrine of reincarnation must be a necessary concomitant of Qabalism. We shall touch on this problem again at the end of this chapter. Perhaps the belief of the magician that completion of the great work – the raising of the microcosm to infinity – demands several lifetimes; (one is manifestly unable to 'hole in one' in this matter) perhaps the allied belief of the Hindu that virtue must be accumulated over many lives in order to escape reincarnation; perhaps both these things and others have contributed to this doctrine's fairly general acceptance.

Crowley undoubtedly believed that he was a reincarnation of Eliphas Levi (an earlier pioneer in this field) and continued where Levi had left off. Crowley met his end *in the midst of an advanced exercise in magical self-deification,* and no doubt, according to his lights, his new incarnation should by now be carrying on the great (if doubtfully good) work. The mind of the magus must compass Kether in his higher visions, and Kether, the crown (of magical endeavour, no doubt) has as its associated virtue, attainment, or the completion of the great work. Its spiritual experience is union with God. (See the appendix to this section.)

It will now help us if we attend to one of the ways in which the Tree of Life is divided into sections. This division is the division into 'four worlds', which are as follows:

> **Atziluth** – The archetypal world
> **Briah** – The creative world
> **Yetzirah** – The formative world
> **Assiah** – The material world

The archetypal world consists of the Sephirah Kether only, the fount and archetype of all things. The creative world consists of the next two Sephiroth, Chokmah and Binah, the pure force and the idea of form from which further creation ensues. The formative world contains the remaining Sephiroth with the exception of Malkuth which is itself the material world.

We must now become clear that, to the Qabalist, *there is a Tree of Life in every Sephirah.* We are, in a sense, able only to comprehend *the Tree in Malkuth.* Each Sephirah is therefore able to be considered with reference to all four 'worlds', and although this may seem to be a complicated and confusing arrangement at first glance, it is fairly obvious and straightforward on reflection. The Tree is the 'plan' of both macrocosm and microcosm.

Each world within a Sephirah has associated with it certain ideas and symbols and colours. In respect of each Sephirah, therefore:

In Atziluth – God is believed to act directly, and there is therefore a God-Name associated with each Sephirah in this world. The names are for the most part Biblical, Hebrew titles appropriate to the Sephirah in question. In the case of Kether, the God-name is Eheieh – 'I am', 'I am that I am', 'I will be that I will be.' (Exod iii. 14)

In Briah – God is believed to act through his archangels, and in this world there is an archangel associated with each

Sephirah. The archangel of Kether is Metatron, whom we met in Chapter Two.

In Yetzirah – God is believed to act through an order of angels, the names of which are Hebrew (and Biblical). In Kether we find Chaioth ha Qadesh, 'Holy living creatures' – a bull, a lion, an eagle and a man. These are the symbols for the four elements, earth, air, fire and water. It will be discovered that the four aces of the tarot – pentacles, swords, wands and cups – the 'roots' of those same four elements, are also associated with Kether.

In Assiah – The Qabalist understands God to act through what is known as the 'Mundane Chakra' – an obscure technical term covering such things as the planets, the elements and the signs of the zodiac. The Mundane Chakra of Kether is called 'First Swirlings' about which Knight maintains, 'This attribution means than an idea of Kether can be gained by going out and contemplating a whirling nebula in the night sky, for it will be an astronomical analogue of the cosmological creation.'⁴

To each Sephirah, and to each World within a Sephirah, is attributed a 'flashing colour', the significance of which is apparent in occult meditation, a subject which will concern us a good deal in a later section of this work. The Appendix at the end of this section will be found to contain a list of the various symbols associated with the Sephiroth and the Worlds as found in the writings of both Dion Fortune and Gareth Knight. It is in meditative and ceremonial magic that these Worlds and their related symbolisms come into their own.

The desire of the sane occultist is self-realization, not only in this world (or incarnation), but final, eternal self-realization. Dion Fortune sees in man, the microcosm, Kether corresponding to the 'thousand-petalled lotus' of Hinduism, the 'Sah' of ancient Egyptian thought, the 'Yechidah' or divine spark of the rabbis. Symbolically, Kether (the crown) is sited not *on* the head but *above* it. The names and traditions quoted convey the same idea, the 'nucleus of pure spirit which emanates *but does not indwell* its many manifestations upon the planes of form [my italics].'⁵ She maintains that, 'never while in incarnation can we rise to the consciousness of Kether in Atziluth and retain the physical vehicle intact against our return. Even as Enoch walked with God and was not, so man that has the vision of Kether is disrupted so far as the vehicle of incarnation is concerned. Why this must be is readily discerned when we remember that we cannot enter into a mode of consciousness save by reproducing it in ourselves, just as music means nothing to us unless the heart sings with it. If therefore we reproduce in ourselves the mode of being of that which has neither form nor activities, it follows that we must free ourselves from form and activity. If we succeed in doing so, that which is held together by the form-mode of consciousness will fall apart and return to its elements. Thus dissolved, it cannot be reassembled by returning consciousness. Therefore when we aspire to the vision of Kether in Atziluth we must be prepared to enter into the Light and come not forth again. This does not imply that Nirvana is annihilation, as an ignorant rendering of Eastern philosophy has taught European thought; but it does imply a complete change of mode of dimension. ... The state of a soul which has attained Nirvana may best be likened to a wheel that has lost its rim and whose spokes have become rays that penetrate and interpenetrate the whole creation; a centre of radiation to whose influence no limit is set save that of its own dynamism, and which maintains its identity as a nucleus of energy.'[6]

There is here a suggestion of the kind of 'communion of saints' which we shall encounter later on, and not specifically connected with Kether. These discarnate beings, the inner plane adepti of the Great White Lodge, are to be met with frequently in obscure references. A number of highly speculative writings in occultism are described thus: 'received from the inner planes through the mediumship of so-and-so'. The Christian will not be over-anxious to endorse such a description and the matter need not detain us now.

Hindu terminology and a doctrine of predestination prepare us for the idea of Karma, which might be described as 'cosmic justice'. In Hinduism, there is no real idea of divine forgiveness; there exists no machinery for it, and the Hindu mind tends to regard the idea as immoral. A frequent complaint against the Christian faith is that God appears to 'condone' sin! Condonation and forgiveness are confused. The Qabalist's dilemma is similar, but – being a kind of 'Western Yoga' – it is more intellectual. Occultism seems bound to the relentless working-out of the implications of the Qabalist mind-system (although all would hotly deny that it is a mind-system!). It is very necessary to remember that the Qabalah is essentially *pre-Christian;* not in terms of history, but in terms of Revelation and human understanding of God. To the Qabalist, God, the great unmanifest, is unknowable; there has not yet come to the occultist *the personal relationship* with God in Christ which, in a very real sense, only a Christian can fully know. The symbol-structure is most profound; the underlying theology is a well-nigh insuperable obstacle as it stands. Before the Qabalah and all it represents can really fulfil its potential for man it needs to be redeemed in Christ, and it is by no means incapable of redemption. Although Dion Fortune was without doubt a Christ-venerating occultist (as many are), *she was equally without doubt a pre-Christian*, and this accounts for a curious lack of dimension, hard to define, in many of her otherwise very shrewd and thoughtful observations.

'The virtue assigned to Kether,' she writes, 'is that of attainment, the completion of the great work, to use a term borrowed from the alchemists. Without completion there can be no attainment, and without attainment no completion. Good intentions weigh light in the scale of cosmic justice; it is by our completed work that we are known. True, we have all eternity in which to complete it, but complete it we must, even to the final Yod. *There is no mercy in perfect justice* [my italics] save that which gives us leave to try again. Kether, viewed from the standpoint of form, is the crown of the kingdom of oblivion. Unless we have realization of the nature of the life of the pure white light we shall have little temptation to strive for the Crown which is not of this order of being at all; and if we have this realization, then are we free from the bondage of manifestation and can speak to all forms as one having authority.' [7]

References

1   Knight, Vol. I, pp. 65-6
2   Knight, Vol. I, p. 66
3   Knight, Vol. I, pp. 66-7
4   Knight, Vol. I, p. 73
5   Fortune, p. 119
6   Fortune, pp. 119-20
7   Fortune, p. 121

Chokmah

The Second path is called the illuminating intelligence. It is the crown of creation, the splendour of unity, equalling it. It is exalted above every head, and is named by Qabalists, the second glory.

THIS Sephirah, the name of which means 'wisdom', is occasionally described as 'the power house'. It is, says Knight, 'The dynamic thrust and drive of spiritual force. It is the upwelling spirit of Kether in positive action ... in its passive aspect Chokmah is a reflection of the primal upwelling of force in Kether, and in its positive aspect it is the divine force in positive function as opposed to its passive mode of action in Binah.'[1] Both Knight and Fortune bid us take the 'point in a void' of Kether, and extend it into a line; a 'point in action'. The straight line is a symbol of Chokmah, as is 'the uplifted rod of power' and a wide selection of Phallic symbolism. Masculinity and primal driving force lie behind the symbols of this Sephirah; it should not be imagined, however, that this is to be understood in a naïve, post-Freudian manner, as human sexuality projected 'upstairs'. We are dealing here with the archetypes of which human sexuality is an expression. This understanding is expressed in the Marriage Service in the Book of Common Prayer; its imagery is important to St Paul, and finds its way into the genuine mysticism of not only Christianity but of every other major world religion.

Of Chokmah, Dion Fortune writes, '... this forth-flowing energy, represented by the straight line or the uplifted rod of power, is essentially dynamic. It is, in fact, the primary dynamism, for we cannot conceive the crystallization of Kether in space as a dynamic process; it partakes rather of a staticism – of the limiting of the formless and free in the bonds of form, tenuous as that form may be in our eyes. The limits of the organization of such a form having been reached, the ever-inflowing force of the unmanifest transcends its limitations, demanding fresh modes of development, establishing fresh relationships and stresses. It is this out-driving of unorganized, uncompensated force which is Chokmah, and because Chokmah is a dynamic Sephirah, ever out-flowing in boundless energy, we do well to look upon it as a channel for the passage of force rather than a receptacle for the storage of force.'[2] This admirable statement puts the idea of Chokmah in a nutshell.

It is worth while attending briefly to the imagery of this Sephirah. The symbolic representation – or 'magical image' – of Chokmah is a bearded male figure, symbolising masculinity and vitality; the phallic imagery quite naturally follows on this. However, the title of the Sephirah – 'wisdom' – is not masculine in Biblical usage, but *feminine*. The correspondences in pagan mythology are also feminine; Pallas-Athene – virgin goddess of wisdom, who sprang from the brow of Zeus rather as Chokmah is understood to have 'sprung' from Kether – and the Egyptian goddess Isis-Urania. The tarot trump assigned to the path between Kether and Chokmah is 'the fool'. He is so called not because of his lack of wits, but because of the motley he wears; the 'inner robe of glory' embroidered with the Tetragrammaton (Name of God), covered with the 'outer robe of concealment', belted with the zodiac (the limitations of time and space). In certain tarot packs the fool is neither man nor woman, but androgyne. The principles of masculinity and femininity are united in God. The 'inner robe' is a symbol of Chokmah, the 'outer robe' is a symbol of Binah. Dion Fortune continues;

'Chokmah is not an organizing Sephirah, but it is the great stimulator of the universe. It is from Chokmah that Binah, the Third Sephirah, receives its influx of emanation, and Binah is the first of the organizing, stabilizing Sephiroth. It is not possible to understand either of the paired Sephiroth without considering its mate; therefore in order to understand Chokmah we shall have to say something about Binah. Let it be noted, then, that Binah is assigned to the planet Saturn and is called the superior mother. In Binah and Chokmah we have the archetypal positive and negative; the primordial maleness and femaleness ... it is from these primary pairs of opposites that the pillars of the universe spring, between which is woven the web of manifestation.'[3]

We shall do well, at this point, to attend to the diagram of 'the pillars' which, if superimposed upon the diagram of the Tree of Life, will link up the three lines of Sephiroth in the vertical plane.

The right-hand pillar, covering from top to bottom, Chokmah, Chesed and Netzach, is called the 'pillar of mercy' and represents the positive principle, the masculine principle, the spiritual principle and the active principle on the various levels of manifestation. With this pillar is associated the ideal of 'force'. The left-hand pillar, covering from top to bottom Binah, Geburah and Hod, is called the 'pillar of severity', and represents the negative, female, material and passive principles, and is associated with the idea of 'form'. This arbitrary, but not unnatural division

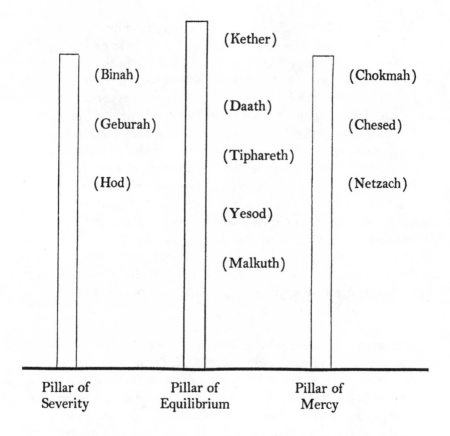

| Pillar of Severity | Pillar of Equilibrium | Pillar of Mercy |

is common to a wide variety of philosophies, outstandingly the 'Yin-Yang' of Chinese Taoism, and there are traces of it in the Old Testament, particularly where the influence of Caananite religion is strongest. The two 'pillars of the temple' feature in masonic symbolism, but the unique feature of the Qabalah is the presence of the middle pillar of equilibrium *or consciousness*, uniting and equilibrating both the opposing principles in itself, and eliminating any idea of dualism, as abhorrent to the Jew as to the monist.

If we may invert the images of horticulture, we may describe the middle pillar as rooted in Kether, the pillar of mercy as rooted in Chokmah, and the pillar of severity as rooted in Binah.

'It may seem strange to uninstructed thought that the title of Mercy should be given to the male or positive pillar, and that of severity to the female pillar; but when it is realised that the dynamic male type of force is the stimulator of upbuilding and evolution, and that the female type of force is the builder of forms, it will be seen that the nomenclature is apt; for form, although it is the builder and organizer, is also the limiter; each form that is built must in turn be outgrown, lose its usefulness, and so become a hindrance to evolving life, and therefore the bringer-in of dissolution and decay, which lead on to death. The father is the giver of life; but the mother is the giver of death, because her womb is the gate of ingress to matter, and through her, life is ensouled in form, and no form can be either infinite or eternal. Death is implicit in birth. It is between these two polarizing aspects of manifestation – the supernal father and the supernal mother – that the web of our life is woven; souls going back and forth between them like a weaver's shuttle. In our individual lives, in our psychological rhythms, and in the history of the rise and fall of nations, we observe the same rhythmic periodicity.'[4]

The Qabalist would see in Genesis i. 27, an admirable illustration of the meaning of the pillars as far as man, the microcosm, is concerned: 'And God created man in his own image, in the image of God created he him; male and female created he them.'

The spiritual experience of Chokmah is the vision of God face to face; and the Virtue associated with the Sephirah is devotion.

'In order to contact Chokmah we must experience the rush of the dynamic cosmic energy in its pure form; an energy so tremendous that mortal man is fused into disruption by it. It is recorded that when Semele, mother of Dionysos, saw Zeus her divine lover in his god-form as the thunderer, she was blasted and burnt, and gave birth to her divine son prematurely. The spiritual experience assigned to Chokmah* is the vision of God face to face; and God ... said to Moses, "Thou canst not look upon my face and live." But although the sight of the divine father blasts mortals with fire, the Divine Son comes familiarly among them and *can be invoked by the appropriate rites* [my italics] – Bacchanalia in the case of the Son of Zeus, and the Eucharist in the case of the Son of Jehovah. Thus we see that there is a lower form of manifestation, which "shows us the father", but that this rite owes its validity solely to the fact that it derives its illuminating intelligence, its inner robe of glory, from the father, Chokmah.'[5]

The underlying Gnosticism in Dion Fortune's philosophy is clear from this last passage. God the Son is an 'emanation on a lower plane' of God the Father; he is 'part of the symbolism'. The Eucharist is not a sacrament – an eternal reality expressed by God in time *through his creation* – but a magical rite performed by man, the microcosm, *invoking higher forces* in the process of raising himself to infinity. The difficulty of the occultist,

---

* *The text says Kether, but this is obviously a misprint, Chokmah is clearly intended.*

his built-in blindness, is the same, be he Western Qabalist or Eastern Hindu; he is a syncretist with an all-embracing system. The Hindu is quite prepared to receive Christ into the Hindu system of devotional 'every-man-for-himself'. Many do. The occultist is at great pains to fit Christ in on the Tree of Life, along with all the other myths and symbols! Neither can see that the Christ demands *unconditional surrender to himself* and the 'burning of books' before, by grace, all the profound truths which emanationism and monism and the Qabalah seek to express, are rediscovered, fulfilled and completed in Christ. The Christ is not a 'system', he is a 'person'. He is not a symbol or an emanation, he is the fulfilment of all these shadows, calling man, not to speculation, *but into a personal relationship* which alone issues in those 'spiritual experiences' which the Qabalists desire. 'Blessed are the pure in heart, for they shall see God' – the experience of Chokmah – and the end of the life of grace is to be with Christ, in God – the experience of Kether.

'As was noted in the chapter upon Kether, the four suits of the tarot pack are assigned to the four elements, and we saw that the four aces represented the roots of the powers of these elements. The four twos are assigned to Chokmah, and represent the polarized functioning of these elements in harmonized balance; therefore a two is always a card of harmony. The two of wands, which is assigned to the element of fire, is called the lord of dominion. The wand is essentially a male phallic symbol, and is attributed to Chokmah, so we may take this card as meaning polarization; the positive that has found its mate in the negative, and is in equilibrium. There is no antagonism or resistance to the lord of dominion, but a contented land accepts his rule; Binah, fulfilled, accepts her mate.

> 'The two of cups (water) is called the lord of love; and here again we have the concept of harmonious polarization. The two of swords (air) is called the lord of peace restored, indicating that the disruptive force of swords is in temporary equilibrium. The two of pentacles (earth) is called the lord of harmonious change. Here, as in swords, we see a modification of the essential nature of the elemental force by its polarizing opposite, thus inducing equilibrium. The disruptive force of swords is restored to peace, and the inertia and resistance of earth becomes, when polarized by the influence of Chokmah, a balanced rhythm.'[6]

The tarot and its mysterious symbolism is a subject on its own. The origins of the tarot are a complete mystery, but it is – or has become – inextricably bound up with the Qabalah in which its every symbol finds a place. The Qabalah is in fact a gigantic card-index system of myth and symbol, everything finding an appropriate place because the Tree of Life is a kind of pattern of fundamental archetypes from which the myths and symbols of man have sprung. Here, in fact, is the great value of the Qabalah and the ample justification for bringing it not only out of obscurity and self-conscious esotericism into the light of day, but also out of darkness and error into the Light of Christ.

The issue of polarity greatly exercises the Qabalist, and continuing her discourse on the four Tarot cards, Dion Fortune maintains, 'these four cards indicate the Chokmah-force in polarity, that is to say the essential balance of power as it manifests in the four worlds of the Qabalists. When they appear in a divination they indicate power in equilibrium. They do not indicate a dynamic force, as might be expected where Chokmah is concerned; because Chokmah, being one of the supernals, its force is positive upon the subtle planes, and consequently negative upon the planes of form.' [7] Dion Fortune enlarges at length upon this, describing the balance of pairs of Sephiroth, not only with each other but throughout the tree by being positively positive, and negatively negative, negatively positive, and so on. At first, or even second reading it gives an impression of hair-splitting pedantry, but reflection discerns more reason and subtlety than is immediately apparent. We shall touch on the subject of divination in a later section of this work but our attention is now claimed by the Third Sephirah of the 'supernal triangle', Binah, whose name means 'understanding'.

References

1   Knight, Vol. I, pp. 76-7
2   Fortune, p. 123
3   Fortune, p. 124
4   Fortune, p. 124
5   Fortune, p. 129
6   Fortune, pp. 135-6
7   Fortune, p. 136

Binah

The third intelligence is called the sanctifying intelligence, the foundation of primordial wisdom; it is also called the creator of faith, and its roots are in amen. It is the parent of faith, whence faith emanates.

WE have already encountered Binah in our brief study of Chokmah. Chokmah is pure 'force', Binah is ideal 'form'; Chokmah is the archetypal male principle, Binah is the archetypal female principle; each completes the other and neither is comprehensible without the other. In Binah, what we may perhaps describe as the 'idea' of manifestation attains balance and coherence. It may seem strange, therefore, that its titles and symbols are sombre; its spiritual experience is 'the vision of sorrow'.

'Wherever there is a state of interacting stresses which have achieved stability, the Qabalists refer the condition to Binah. For instance the atom, being for all practical purposes the stable unit of the physical plane, is a manifestation of the Binah type of force,' says Dion Fortune. 'All social organizations on which the dead hand of unprogressiveness weighs heavily, such as the Chinese civilization before the revolution, or our older universities, are said to be under the influence of Binah. To Binah are attributed the Greek god Chronos (who is none other than Father Time) and the Roman god Saturn. It will be observed the importance attached to time, in other words to age, in these Binah institutions; only grey hairs are venerable; ability alone carries little weight ... Binah, the great mother, sometimes also called Marah, the great sea, is, of course, the Mother of All Living. She is the archetypal womb through which life comes into manifestation. Whatsoever provides a form to serve life as a vehicle is of her. It must be remembered, however, that life confined in a form, although it is enabled thereby to organize and so evolve, is much less free than it was when it was unlimited (though also unorganized) on its own plane. Involvement in a form is therefore the beginning of the death of life. It is a straightening and a limiting; a binding and a constricting. Form checks life, thwarts it, and yet enables it to organize. Seen from the point of view of free-moving force, incarnation in a form is extinction. Form disciplines force with a merciless severity. The disembodied spirit is immortal; there is nothing of it that can grow old or die. But the embodied spirit sees death on the horizon as soon as its day dawns. We can see then how terrible must the great mother appear as she binds free-moving force into the discipline of form. She is death to the dynamic activity of Chokmah; the Chokmah-force dies as it issues into Binah. Form is the discipline of force; therefore is Binah the head of the pillar of severity.'[1]

The insights expressed by Dion Fortune are profound, and, to the Christian, very largely valid. The self-emptying of our Lord at his Incarnation (known to certain theologians as 'kenosis') can be expressed very well in Dion Fortune's terms – although still inadequately, and still subject to the limitations of the finite human mind. The womb of the Blessed Virgin Mary was in a very real sense a gateway to death for her divine Son. From the moment of his 'taking flesh' his death was a certainty. The Incarnate Lord was bound to die by very virtue of his incarnation. Indeed, he became incarnate *in order to die*. But the Qabalistic framework will not fit all the way; our faith tells us that our Lord became man, 'not by conversion of godhead into flesh: but by taking manhood into God'. Our Lord was born in order to die, it is true; but it is also true that he died in order to be raised from the dead. Our Lord will not fit into the Tree of Life; it must fit into him!

The imagery of Binah is strikingly appropriate to our Lady; this is to be expected because the whole of the incarnation represented the fulfilment of fundamental, archetypal images which are expressed in numerous ways and in virtually every religious system.

'Binah is the form giver to all manifestation and thus also is the Archetypal temple behind all temples, the inner church behind all churches, the basic creed behind all creeds,' claims Gareth Knight. 'It is the womb of Life, and this archetypal feminine quality of the Sephirah manifests in two aspects, as Ama, the dark sterile mother, and Aima, the bright fertile mother ... Ama, the dark mother, is the aspect of Binah which binds the free-moving force of Chokmah into limiting form. Aima tends more to the future condition when the imprisoned force has achieved harmonized function in form and the form is therefore no longer a necessary limitation for its development. ... It must not be forgotten that the spiritual side of the Ama power is part of the action of the cosmic Christ, the regenerating and reconciling aspect of God. Regeneration could be defined as the facing up to individual reality honestly combined with the genuine desire to change. It can be a painful process for the personality; few people care to look at their failings honestly, and many fear change of any kind as it appears to be a threat to security. The dross in human nature goes up in flames when exposed to this regenerative fire, and the dark Mother, the mother of sorrows, who mediates this force to the character over a greater or lesser period of time is really a figure of great compassion compared to the direct application of a cosmic force as potent as the cosmic Christ, the searing heat of which, applied to the soul, would be akin to applying an oxy-acetylene torch to the body. *The cosmic Christ force should not be confused with the Lord Jesus, the master of compassion* [my italics]. What is meant here is the blind cosmic force which was mediated in one of its greatest forms in the history of mankind by our Lord in his capacity as the bearer of the Christ force. The Lord Jesus mediates this force as does the Ama figure, which is represented in Christian worship as the Virgin Mary ... the *"Mater Dolorosa"*. And her description in the Litany as *"Mater Boni Consilii"* is very apt for the understanding of Binah.'[2]

There is a great deal to think about in this passage. Images of the less generally accepted Christian titles of our Lady as 'co-redemptrix' and 'mediatrix of all graces' come speedily to mind. We are reminded of the aberrational view of our Lady as the gentle mediatrix, interceding on behalf of man with a severe Christ. We see in Knight's passage something of the subconscious origins of such an idea, wholly at variance though it is with the entire New Testament, and wholly false though it is to the whole spirit of the Gospel. Our Lady fulfils all the types and shadows, transcends them and transforms them. The pre-Christian mediatrix, such as Kuan Yin, the Chinese goddess of mercy, is appropriate only to a pre-Christian world. In Christ, man is redeemed and *taken up into God*. The whole relationship between God the Creator and creation, summed up in man, is wholly and eternally transformed in Christ. Man needs no mediator save the Christ of whom, by baptism, the Christian is a part – a member of his body, the Church. The Church is the world's priest because she is the body of the eternal Christ. The prayer which has been added to the *Ave Maria:* 'Holy Mary, Mother of God, pray for us sinners, now and at the hour of our death,' is not a prayer to a pre-Christian mediatrix, be she an Ama or an Aima figure. It is a request for Christian intercession, and when a Christian makes intercession, *he shares in Christ's love for the subject of his intercession.* The Christ prays – loves – through the Christian, by the Christian's deliberate conformity of his will, by grace. There is, in the Christ, no separation of the 'living' and the 'dead', no sundering of an eternal fellowship. The Christian's request for our Lady's prayers is the request of one member of the body of another; a mutual love-sharing in Christ. The Qabalah is pre-Christian and its limitations must not be lost sight of.

We shall encounter the Qabalistic idea of Christ later on in our examination of Tiphareth; but the description of our Lord as bearer of a 'blind cosmic Christ-force' is one with which no Christian will feel at ease! The idea is at once consistent with the emanationism of the Qabalah, and at the same time, oddly out of place in it. Why, in such a universe as the Qabalist visualizes, is a 'Christ-force' required? Why must an emanated cosmos in which 'there is no part of me which is not part of the gods', be redeemed? What has gone wrong – what can have gone wrong – with the microcosm that it should need redemption? The question does not find a really satisfactory answer.

The Qabalists (or some at any rate) acknowledge a fall. This is a matter of observation and experience, and it is the one untidy fact which spoils an otherwise faultlessly ordered system. Knight's remarks about regeneration are apt if thought of in terms of repentance. Confronted with the awful purity of Christ, the sinful human soul is blasted, as those who have known the experience of sensible conversion are aware. The fall is explained variously by Qabalists; some see a Platonic arrangement of a 'perfect tree' of which this is an imperfect replica; others see a dislocation having taken place below the three supernal Sephiroth. The doctrine of the Fall is, even for Christians, difficult of satisfactory definition, so we may simply acknowledge the end-result in common with the Qabalists; man is fallen and is in need of redemption. The Christ-force is (for the Qabalist) the redeeming agent and it is mediated in the Sephirah Tiphareth by various redeemers, of which our Lord is – for some at least – the chief.

The occultist, the 'Western Hindu', is as ever incurably syncretistic.

'The manifestation of sorrow in the human personality can be regarded as the work of Ama, the mother of sorrows. Grief is a purgative and strongly disruptive force, and when the essential work of breaking down adhesions and dispersing poisons has been done by it, it gives place to a deep lassitude and feeling of emptiness which can act as a purified basis for new growth. People are so made that they will not or cannot realize a thing fully unless they are hit in the most vital part in some deep emotional sense. And so only by sorrow and by going from sorrow to sorrow can an individual's evolution proceed. The man who cannot or will not feel sorrow or face it in others cannot proceed at all. There is, however, no value in grief for its own sake. Through some quirk of the human make-up it tends to be regarded as a static image instead of a process which leads on to a higher level of enlightenment and rest and thus transformed from a negative destructive force into a positive constructive one. *Exoteric Christianity has tended to make this mistake and become fixated in the Crucifixion without going on to the subsequent Resurrection and Ascension.*' [3]

Knight's words in this passage express much profound truth of which many Christians, who of all people should know better, have undoubtedly lost sight. It is, alas, only too manifestly true that the faith and devotion of much of the Western Church has seemed to stop short at the crucifixion. An exaggerated devotion to the passion, subjective and self-regarding, was a most marked feature of the time of the Reformation, and partly the cause of it. It is only in quite recent years that this melancholy tendency has begun to give place to a more obviously balanced and healthy approach. *The Imitation of Christ*, a classic of devotion, written at the height of this passion-centred period, clearly reflects the shortcomings which Knight very rightly condemns. Here, as elsewhere, we find the Qabalist repelled, not by the Christian faith, but by the failure of Christians to hold it in its fulness!

> 'If one should be undergoing a period of grief it can be of great help in more ways than one to picture the mother of sorrows. ... This figure can be considered as Christian or pagan, for the sorrow of the feminine side of divinity is the same throughout the ages, whether it be Demeter sorrowing for her daughter, Ishtar descending the seven hells for her lover, Isis searching for the dismembered parts of her husband, or Mary watching her son die. On the higher levels the sorrow of Binah is the knowledge and understanding of the great cosmic factors behind the incarnation of man and also of Christ. It is the realization and revelation of the great mother herself. An awareness of this condition can be made by building the picture of the crucifixion with our Lady and St John on either side of the cross ... This image should lead to an understanding of the whole of the manifested universe as a form encompassing pure cosmic force; a gigantic cross upon which this force is crucified. And the whole of life is lived under the shadow of this cross. This is the primary cross of Life of which the cross of Golgotha is a lesser manifestation; a shadow cast by the great shadow.' [4]

A very deep understanding of the cross is evident here, and yet it is not quite a Christian understanding. The cross is indeed in the heart of God, and Calvary was indeed the expression in time and for all time of that eternal reality, which – Christians affirm – is continually expressed throughout time on the altars of the Church. This is not quite the same thing as the cross of Golgotha being a 'lesser manifestation' of the primary cross of Life; but the Christian will nevertheless see these insights at least as being 'not far from the Kingdom of Heaven'.

When we attend to the various symbols attributed to this Sephirah, we find the 'God-name', 'Jehovah (Yahweh) Elohim' exhibiting features which we might expect; Elohim is a feminine word with a masculine ending, and the unity of male and female principles in God is proclaimed thereby. The archangel, however, is a stranger to us. His name is Tzaphkiel and like Metatron he is new to Bible scholars. His function is an important one in Qabalist eyes, because he is in charge of the machinery of reincarnation and all that that implies. Of Tzaphkiel, Knight says, 'The archangel of Binah has been called the "keeper of the records of evolution" and as the influence of Binah develops forms from the Akashic sea of consciousness, which is the basic matter of life; this presumably has reference to the cosmic Akashic records, the memory of God which records all things that occur during the course of manifestation. ... Thus the archangel Tzaphkiel, in that all the karmic records are under his jurisdiction, is a higher analogue of the dark angel of the soul of man who mediates the Ama force of discipline and regeneration to him, just as the archangel of Chokmah, Ratziel, represents archetypally the bright angel of the Soul of Man who brings illumination and guidance ... the dark angel holds the repository of a soul's karma and the bright angel its destiny. Destiny is the task the spirit undertook to carry out on entry into manifestation, and karma is the action necessary, often painful, to readjust past errors that have occurred through the fall of man in order that he shall be in a position to take up his work of destiny – to return his hand to the plough. On the tree used as a chart of the psychology of man, these two personal angels are usually ascribed to the spheres of Chesed and Geburah. The archangel Tzaphkiel can also be considered to preside over all the planes of the cosmos, just as Ratziel, the archangel of Chokmah, presides over the cosmic rays, whose analogues are the zodiacal signs. Tzaphkiel could also be considered as the Altar of Manifestation and Ratziel as the fires of creative force descending upon it. And, as this attribution implies, Tzaphkiel is behind the formulation of all the mystical groups that have emanated from the Great White Lodge. He is the archangel of the archetypal temple.'[5]

At first sight, the virtue and the vice associated with the Sephirah Binah seem arbitrary, but on reflection this is seen not to be so. Avarice, the vice, is concerned with obsession with form. Binah is the form behind all forms. Knight interprets avarice as the 'vice behind all vices', but his interpretation seems really to be a description of pride which, the Christian would agree, is indeed the 'primordial vice' if such a term can be permitted. 'The virtue of Binah is silence and this implies silence on all levels of being, not only the physical. It is necessary to still all the clamouring noises of the lower levels in order to hear the voice of the spirit, and so the ideal state of form in order to make the vertical contacts is one of quietude. On another more practical level, if one is performing magical work and building up forms in subtle matter, silence and secrecy are essential in order not to break the psychic stresses. The easiest way to ruin esoteric work is to talk about it, and as Binah is the Archetypal temple where forms are built for forces to indwell, it is natural that the virtue should be silence. The virtue is exemplified in the great Binah figure of the Virgin Mary – she who knew the wonderful and terrible experiences beyond the esoteric knowledge and experience of any ordinary woman and could sufficiently possess the inner wisdom to keep all such things to herself.'[6]

It will be worth our while to hear Dion Fortune, on the subject of the tarot as found in Binah.

'The four threes of the tarot pack are the cards assigned to Binah, and indeed the number three is intimately associated with the idea of manifestation in matter. The two opposing forces find expression in a third, the equilibrium between them, which manifests on a lower plane than its parents. The triangle is one of the symbols assigned to Saturn as the god of densest matter, and the triangle of art, as it is called, is used in magical ceremonies when it is the intention to evoke a spirit to visible appearance on the plane of matter; for other modes of manifestation, a circle is used. The three of wands is called the lord of established strength. Here again we have the idea of power in equilibrium, which is so characteristic of Binah. Wands, be it remembered, represents the dynamic Yod force. This force, when in the sphere of Binah, ceases to be dynamic and becomes consolidated. Cups are essentially the female force, for the cup or chalice is one of the symbols of Binah and is intimately allied with the yoni in esoteric symbolism. The three of cups is, therefore, at home in Binah, for the two sets of symbolism reinforce each other. The three of cups, which is aptly named abundance, represents the fertility of Binah in her Ceres aspect. The three of swords, however, is called Sorrow, and its symbol in the tarot pack is a heart pierced by three swords. Our readers will recall the reference to the sword-pierced heart of the Virgin Mary in Catholic symbolism, and Mary equates with Marah, bitter, the sea "Ave, Maria, stella maris!" Swords are of course, Geburah cards, and as such represent the destructive aspect of Binah as Kali, the wife of Siva, the Hindu goddess of destruction. Pentacles are cards of earth, and as such are congenial to Binah, form. The three of pentacles, therefore, is lord of material Works, or activity on the plane of form.'[7]

We have now arrived at the completion of the first of the three ' triangles' on the tree which we encountered, briefly, in Chapter Two. It is the 'archetypal or supernal triangle' of Kether, Chokmah and Binah. The tree is made up of three such triangles, of which the second is the 'moral or ethical triangle' of Chesed, Geburah and Tiphareth. This in turn manifests on a lower arc as the 'Astral or psychological – or magical – triangle' of Netzach, Hod and Yesod. From this last triangle, the physical world – Malkuth – hangs as a kind of pendant.

The three triangles have a correspondence in the microcosm, man.

'Briefly, the human being can be divided for purposes of analysis into three vehicles: the part of him which is eternal, the part of him that lasts as long as an evolution, and the part of him that lasts only a human lifetime in earth. The first we will call the spirit, the second the individuality, and the third the personality. The spirit, when it enters the manifest universe, has its own spiritual vehicle which projects into denser manifestation an evolving unit which we call the individuality. This in turn projects into even denser manifestation *a series of personalities* [my italics] with which it gains experience of dense, worldly life. Qabalistically, the spirit can be assigned to the Sephirothic triangle of Kether, Chokmah and Binah; the individuality to Chesed, Geburah and Tiphareth; and the personality to Netzach, Hod and Yesod, the actual physical body being represented by Malkuth. There is also a certain amount of overlap in the linking Sephiroth of Daath and Tiphareth. The personality can aspire to and touch Tiphareth in its higher moments as the individuality can with Daath. Similarly the spirit can reach down to Daath.'[8]

The vision of man thus presented is both dark and strange to the Christian, presupposing, as it does, the doctrine of reincarnation. But we must go on now to examine the strange, 'hidden' Sephirah called Daath, or 'knowledge', before we can proceed with the second triangle on the tree.

References

1   Fortune, pp. 142-3
2   Knight, Vol. I, pp. 90-1
3   Knight, Vol. I, pp. 93-4
4   Knight, Vol. I, pp. 94-5
5   Knight, Vol. I, pp. 96-7
6   Knight, Vol. I, p. 99
7   Fortune, pp. 159-60
8   Knight, Vol. II, p. iv

Daath

THERE is no 'Yetziratic Text' to head this short chapter. The Sephirah Daath has been reckoned among the Sephiroth only in recent times. In place of our usual text we may perhaps take a part of Mathers' translation of another esoteric work called the *Greater Holy Assembly* which Dion Fortune quotes: 'From the third cavity there goes forth a thousand times a thousand conclaves and assemblies, wherein Daath, knowledge, is contained and dwelleth. And the hollow place of this cavity is between the other two cavities; and all these conclaves are filled from either side. This is that which is written in Proverbs, "And in knowledge (Daath) shall the conclaves be filled." And those three are expanded over the whole body, on this side and on that, and with them does the whole body cohere, and the body is contained by them on every side, and through the whole body are they expanded and diffused.'

We may feel none the wiser after reading this, but Dion Fortune continues, 'When it is recalled that Daath is situated at the point where the Abyss bisects the middle pillar, and that up the middle pillar lies the path of the arrow, the way by which consciousness goes when the psychic rises on the planes, and that here also is Kundalini, we see that in Daath is the secret of both generation and regeneration, the key to the manifestation of all things through the differentiation into pairs of opposites and their union in a third.'[1] The Qabalist is hard put to it to explain what he means by Daath.

The 'abyss' is the gulf fixed between what Qabalists call macroprosopos (otherwise known as the 'vast countenance') and microprosopos (or the 'lesser countenance'). It is not quite true to equate these ideas with God and man respectively; the first has to do with the supernals and the second with the remainder of the Sephiroth. The distinction is really between 'celestial man' and 'terrestrial (or evolving) man'. The Sephirah Daath is in the Abyss that separated the two concepts.

In her book *The Mystical Qabalah*, from which much is quoted in this work, Dion Fortune, who devotes a chapter apiece to the other Sephiroth, has none for Daath. Daath is encountered throughout her book, however. Crowley suggests that it should really be thought of as being in another dimension to the Sephiroth, but this idea will not help us much. Gareth

Knight, however, devotes a chapter to it, and it is from him that we shall learn the most in our present study.

'Daath,' says Knight, 'is the sphere where pure force takes on a form. Binah represents the archetypal idea of form and the fourth Sephirah, Chesed, is a Sephirah of forms; Daath represents the state where actual forms are precipitated from the interaction of supernal forces. Daath could thus be conceived of as a lower analogue of Kether, but a state where form and not force first manifests. The forms implied here are of course in still a very abstract condition, being more in the nature of nodes of energy. Actual images and shapes as we generally understand them do not occur until the Sephirah Hod.'[2]

Concerning the microcosm, he continues, 'Daath is the highest point of awareness of the human soul regarded as a soul (or in other terminologies higher self, evolutionary self, etc.), for awareness of the supernal levels can only be possible to the spirit or divine spark itself. It is the gateway to what is called Nirvana in the East, and thus represents the point where a soul has reached the full stature of its evolutionary development, has attained perfect free will and can make the choice between *going on to further evolution in other spheres or remaining to assist in the planetary Hierarchy* [my italics]. ... Before the grade of Daath the experience of a soul is devoted to bringing about a fusion of itself with the spirit – to "becoming". After the powers of Daath are fully operative in a soul there is no further process of "becoming" for that soul "*is*".'[3]

It will be worth our while to reflect upon the progression of ideas contained in the names of the previous two Sephiroth and this present one; the names are first 'wisdom', then 'understanding' and now 'knowledge'. There is a steady concretion, a growing 'tangibility' evident in this progression. Daath has been called the mystical Sephirah, and has been claimed to bring about a right understanding of this much-bandied word 'mysticism', which Knight would define as a clear-cut realization of the various potencies of life and their unity with God and with the soul. This is not a definition that the Christian can be entirely happy with; it fits the Qabalist usage, but not the Christian experience. The Christian would define mysticism as, 'in general, an immediate knowledge of God attained in this present life through personal religious experience. It is primarily a state of prayer. ... The surest proof adduced by the mystics themselves for the genuineness of their experience is its effect, viz. its fruit in such things as an increase of humility, charity, and love of suffering. ... Distinctive of the Christian form of mysticism is its emphasis on two elements often absent elsewhere. In contrast to all pan-cosmic conceptions of the underlying reality as an impersonal Unity, it recognizes that the reality to which it penetrates transcends the soul and the cosmos. And in place of all notions of absorption of the soul into the divine … it posits *that the union is one of love and will in which the distinction between creator and creature is permanently maintained.*[4] The Christian and the Qabalist, in speaking of mysticism, are not talking about quite the same thing; the distinction between the two understandings is of the first importance.

'In Christian language,' Knight continues, 'Daath is the sphere of the upper room at the descent of the Pentecostal flames. In pre-Christian times it was the sphere of the creative fire in the realm of mind. For example in Druidism it was connected with Beltane, though Beltane was the festival of the earthly creative fire as well. The symbol of the cloudhidden peak of the sacred mountain of any race is apposite to Daath for it was Daath consciousness that Moses contacted when he received the Tables of the Law from the top of Sinai, the moon mountain. This consciousness could be shown under the symbol of a grain of corn – the sense of being *in* everything, containing, in essence, the sacramental bread. Daath, then, is the sphere of realization in its supremest meaning, understanding united with knowledge – and those two words are chosen with care. The human mind at this most abstract level attains to a complete awareness of All and in this complete awareness is absorbed by the eternal mind and made one with it, so that Daath, as a Sephirah, represents supreme wisdom and supreme power of realization. And realization at its greatest height is illumination, and all the supernal revelations of ancient times that have come to great spiritual leaders have been acquired through contact with the consciousness attributed to Daath.'[5]

The insights expressed here are very profound indeed, and the Christian will be all the more saddened by the fact that the Qabalist's interpretation seems fated to be forever 'just missing the boat'. There is a kind of chest-constricting frustration attendant upon every profound insight – and there are many.

The reason is not hard to find; everything has to be fitted into a closed system and the Christian mystic, who has a wholly other dimension to his mystical consciousness, sees the various flashes of illumination turned inexorably back to be imprisoned within the ball-and-chain system of the Tree of Life. The Christian, approaching the Qabalah in charity and with an open mind, will see here a great 'tool' which he can take into his hands and use to the glory of God. But it is like a net in many ways. A fisherman can become prisoner in his own net, as is the Qabalist. Everything is 'symbolism' to be hung on the tree, the great pattern of archetypes. The Qabalist cannot really grasp the understanding that the Christ has transcended and fulfilled every symbol that the tree contains.

Only the Christ – and the Christian in the Christ – can take the 'net' into his hands and catch fish with it. The Qabalist can only flounder in its folds, because, despite which century it is in which he is currently incarnate, he is a pre-Christian; he cannot release himself, he must *be released*.

Daath has to do with the Qabalistic concept of absolute justice. It is interesting to see that the virtues and vices assigned to this 'middle pillar' Sephirah are not so much opposites as states of balance (virtues) and states of virtues out of balance (vices). The Daath powers on balance give a sense of mission and a sufficient sense of detachment to enable the mission to be fulfilled. In a state of imbalance, these powers produce fanaticism, which is self-destructive. It is a parody of a right sense of mission and of the integrity which chooses death before dishonour or compromise.

Knight draws a clear distinction between the self-chosen deaths of our Lord, of Socrates and of the likes of Thomas More, and the fanatical 'Ragnarokk' of Adolf Hitler. 'Evil always pays good the compliment of masquerading as it, but the unfailing diagnostic indicator of it is lack of compassion, or, those other much misunderstood terms, charity, humanity, or the love of God.'[6]

Knight's practical concerns, as far as the Tree of Life is concerned, are with what we may describe as 'meditative magic', a subject which we will examine later on. He warns against meditation on Daath without due care, and makes much of the colour symbolism unique to Qabalistic meditation. The Isis myths are the best, he claims, for attaining an understanding of the brighter, positive side to this Sephirah. The darker side is illustrated in the myths of Prometheus, Galahad and Perseus.

He concludes his chapter with the reminder that, 'all attempts at a description of the states of consciousness of Daath can at best be only metaphorical, for really it is the state of awareness devoid of all symbols. … It is a "condition" beyond all other conditions – a Supreme State, and this state is approached when the phase of the abstract mind is entered. The approach to this state, which can be analysed into several stages, is along a "secret" path of the Tree of Life, from Chesed towards Daath. It is an initiatory process for the *Adeptus Exemptus* – one who has learned all that earth has to teach – and the way can be a terrible one, being the well known dark night of the soul of the mystic, but on a higher arc than is usually experienced.'[7]

We shall encounter references to St John of the Cross, and to the dark nights, when we come to consider occult meditation. The parallels between Qabalistic Paths and St John's teachings are close, but the all important difference is one of *dimension;* his teachings are interpreted *within the Qabalah*, where he does not belong and where his teaching, though superficially apt, simply does not fit.

References

1 Fortune, pp. 47-8
2 Knight, Vol. I, p. 102
3 Knight, Vol. I, pp. 102-3
4 The Oxford Dictionary of the Christian Church
5 Knight, Vol. I, pp. 103-4
6 Knight, Vol. I, p. 105
7 Knight, Vol. I, p. 112

Chesed

The fourth path is called the cohesive or receptive intelligence because it contains all the holy powers, and from it emanate all the spiritual virtues with the most exalted essences. They emanate one from another by virtue of the primordial emanation, the highest crown, Kether.

'WE can learn much from the position of a Sephirah in the pattern of the tree,' says Dion Fortune, 'and from the position of Chesed on the pillar of mercy we see that it is Chokmah upon a lower arc. It is emanated by Binah, a passive Sephirah, and emanates Geburah, a katabolic Sephirah, whose Mundane Chakra is Mars with all his warlike symbolism, who is Saturn upon a lower arc. From these we can learn a great deal about Chesed. It is the loving father, the protector and preserver, just as Chokmah is the all-begetter. It continues the work of Chokmah, organizing and preserving that which the All-Father has begotten. It balances with mercy the severity of Geburah. It is anabolic, or upbuilding, in contradistinction to the katabolism, or down-breaking of Geburah. ... Chesed, being the first Sephirah of microprosopos, or the manifested universe, represents the formulation of the archetypal idea, the concretion of the abstract. When the abstract principle that forms the root of some new activity is formulating in our minds, we are operating in the sphere of Chesed.'[1]

Dion Fortune illustrates this vividly by describing the imaginings of an explorer looking over a newly discovered piece of country and visualizing the gradual settlement, growth of civilization and the industrial society that will one day be there. The creative work of the world is done, she maintains, by minds who work in terms of Chesed, whose magical image is a mighty king, crowned and enthroned, ruling and guiding his people.

Of those people whose minds cannot function at a higher level than Malkuth, the physical world, she says, 'they are the folk who cannot see the wood for the trees. They think in terms of detail, lacking any synthetic principle. Their logic is never able to reach back to origins but is always materialistic. ... The occultist who does not possess the initiation of Chesed will be limited in his function to the sphere of Yesod, the plane of Maya, illusion. For him the astral images reflected in the magic mirror of subconsciousness will be actualities; he will make no attempt to translate them into terms of a higher plane and learn what they really represent. He will have made himself a dwelling in the sphere of illusion, and he will be deluded by the phantasms of his own unconscious projection. If he were able to function in terms of Chesed, he would perceive the underlying archetypal ideas of which these magical images are but the shadows and symbolic representations. He then becomes a master in the treasure-house of images instead of being hallucinated by them. He can use the images as a mathematician uses algebraic symbols. He works magic as an initiated adept and not as a magician. The mystic functioning in the Christ centre of Tiphareth, if he lacks the keys of Chesed, will also be hallucinated but in a different and more subtle way. Upon this level he will read the magical images truly enough, referring them to that which they represent and giving them no values save as tokens, as St Theresa has so clearly shown in her "interior castle". *He will fall into the error, however, of thinking that the images he perceives and the experiences he undergoes are the direct and personal dealings of God with his soul, instead of realising that they are stages on the path.* He will find a personal saviour in the God-man instead of in the regenerative influence of the Christ-force. *He will worship Jesus of Nazareth as God the Father,* thus confounding the persons [my italics].' [2]

The idea of Chesed is clearly outlined, and the impossibility of comprehending Christian mysticism in Qabalistic terms is also clear. Dion Fortune, a clear-thinking, perceptive woman, and in many ways an attractive personality in her writings, exhibits a fundamental lack of understanding of the Christian faith in its fulness. This we see clearly manifested throughout her writings.

But there is always something in her strictures for the Christian to recognize as deserving of sympathy. To what extent, we may wonder, did a naïve, sentimental 'Jesus-worship' of a popular Protestantism more common in her generation than ours, repel her? Was her experience of the faith limited to an introspective and inhibited piety which was fundamentally unsatisfying to such a temperament? Or did she never really have any first-hand knowledge of the Christian religion in any adult form? We do not know, but the symptoms manifested are both interesting and sad.

Chesed is the sphere in which archetypal ideas begin to be apprehended by the consciousness of the microcosm, and are 'concreted'. In its macrocosmic aspect it represents a corresponding phase in the process of creation. In following the idea of Chesed further, we shall encounter, almost at once, a Qabalistic concept of a kind of 'communion of saints' which we have already met, very briefly. Chesed is the sphere of the 'masters'. The concept of the masters is entirely strange to the Christian, and we must look to our teachers, Knight and Fortune, for enlightenment.

The history of the masters is described by Knight as 'stormy'. Before the nineteenth century they were rarely mentioned, and Knight warns against trying to imagine them too anthropomorphically, in spite of the fact that they are *human*.

> 'The masters, as we picture them, are images in our imagination, as indeed are all inner plane entities, human, angelic or elemental. But this does not mean that they are the product of our imaginations. They are real beings on their own level. And the level of the masters corresponds to the Sephirah Chesed, which is a sphere where forms are of the density of the processes of the abstract mind or intuition.' [3]

After a sharp warning against romanticism and an over-heated imagination, Knight continues:

> 'The masters, or inner plane adepti, are human beings who have gained all the experience, and all the wisdom resulting from experience, necessary for their spiritual evolution in the worlds of form. They are thus "just men made perfect". All souls, when they have become free of the necessity for birth and death, can go on to higher evolution in other spheres, but some elect to stay behind in earth conditions in order to help on their "younger brethren" in their progress through cyclic evolution on this planet. These are the Masters, and there are many of them, though only a few are known to humanity by name for it is only the "teaching masters" who communicate directly with us. It is this "college of masters" that forms the upper reaches of the *planetary hierarchy of human beings,* [my italics] just as the archangels form the upper reaches of the angelic and elemental hierarchy. The function of the masters is to mediate divine forces, or the will of God, to humanity and thus can they be considered to operate in the Sephirah Chesed. The "inner council of masters", however, commonly referred to as "The Great White Lodge" is more of a Daath condition, for when a "council" is in full session the contacts with the higher supernal levels are made and with unnameable and unknowable beings who have their existence in those remote spheres. *It must be remembered that these terms are at best approximate* [my italics] and that the nature of the "council" and its higher contacts is more in the fashion of a high telepathic rapport than a council meeting as we commonly understand it.' [4]

Dion Fortune elucidates further, describing the work of these unexpected beings as the concretion of the abstract ideas of the 'logoidal consciousness'.

There is a tradition in occultism which relates the world of men as we know it to the solar system, under the ultimate presidency of what is known as a solar logos. Sirius, the dog-star, is spoken of as the 'sun behind our sun'. This Gnostic pile-up of systems upon systems and planes upon planes is an indication of the desperate 'unknowability' of the unknowable – who is pushed ever further away by the mind of the Qabalist, whose doctrine of 'a tree in every Sephirah' enables such a process to fit into the Qabalistic system. Of this 'logos', Dion Fortune writes: 'The logos, whose meditation gives birth to worlds and whose unfolding consciousness is evolution conceives archetypal ideas out of the substance of the unmanifest – to use a metaphor where definition is impossible. These ideas remain within the cosmic consciousness of the logos like the seed within the flower, because there is no soil therein for their germination. The logoidal consciousness, as pure being, cannot upon its own plane provide the formative aspect necessary for manifestation. It is taught in the esoteric traditions that the masters, discarnate consciousnesses disciplined by form but now formless, in their meditations upon the Godhead are able to perceive telepathically these archetypal ideas in the mind of God, and by realizing the practical application of them to the planes of form and the line this development will follow, produce concrete images in their own consciousness which serve to bring the abstract archetypal ideas down to the first of the planes of form, called by the Qabalists, Briah.'

The whole construction is remarkable, and Dion Fortune continues, 'This, then, is the work that the masters perform in their special sphere, the sphere of the organizing, upbuilding, constructive Chesed on the pillar of mercy. The work of the dark masters, who are quite different from the black adepts, is performed in the corresponding sphere of Geburah, on the pillar of severity, which will be considered in due course. The point of contact between the masters and their human disciples is in Hod, the Sephirah of ceremonial magic, as is indicated by the Yetziratic Text, which declares that from Gedulah, the fourth Sephirah emanates the essence of Hod. ... Hod, then, may be taken as representing Chokmah and Chesed upon a lower arc, even as Netzach represents Binah and Geburah. This will be explained in detail when these Sephiroth are dealt with, but it must be referred to now in order to make the function of Chesed intelligible.'[6]

Chesed and the masters – strange though these beings seem to the Christian – are inseparable in Qabalistic thought, as reflection will reveal. If no masters existed in the Qabalistic scheme of things, then they would have had to have been invented (the same has been said of Moses by Biblical scholars!) and perhaps their 'invention' (the word means 'discovery') was the occasion of their late arrival on the Qabalistic scene and their stormy advent.

Chesed represents the first point in our descent down the tree where the activity comes within the range of human consciousness. 'It is to the sphere of Chesed that the exalted consciousness of the adept rises in his occult meditations; it is here that he receives the inspirations which he works out on the planes of form. It is here that he meets the masters as spiritual influences contacted telepathically, without any intermingling of personality. This is the true, and the highest, mode of contact with the masters, contact with them as mind to mind in their own sphere of exalted consciousness.'[6]

The symbols and attributes of this Sephirah all bear out its place on the pillar of mercy. Stability, order, merciful law, all come under the image of the benevolent king which is its magical image. The Mundane Chakra is Jupiter, the benign. Its associated vices are all vices against ordered society. The alternative title of this Sephirah – one Dion Fortune frequently uses – is Gedulah, meaning 'love'. It is worth noting that the meaning of the word Chesed in the book of the prophet Hosea is 'loving kindness', which is a better title and a better understanding of the meaning of this interesting Sephirah.

Finally, let us attend to the tarot:

'The four tarot cards that are placed on Chesed when the pack is set up for a divination carry out the ruling idea in the correspondence. The four of wands symbolizes perfected work, thus representing admirably the achievement of the king in peace-time in his well-governed kingdom. The four of cups is called the lord of pleasure, and is in keeping with the title of splendour assigned to Chesed and with the brilliancy of its angelic host. The four of swords indicates rest from strife, and agrees perfectly with the significance of the seated ruler. The four of pentacles is the lord of earthly power, a symbolism so obvious that it needs no elucidation.'[7]

References

1   Fortune, pp. 162-3
2   Fortune, pp. 164-5
3   Knight, Vol. I, p. 115
4   Knight, Vol. I, p. 117
5   Fortune, pp. 166-7
6   Fortune, p. 168
7   Fortune, p. 171

Geburah

The fifth path is called the radical intelligence because it resembles unity, uniting itself to Binah, understanding, which emanates from the primordial depths of Chokmah, wisdom.

THE Sephirah Geburah need not detain us long. Its name means 'severity' and its two alternative titles are Pachad, meaning 'fear' and Din, meaning 'justice'. In the midst of the Pillar of Severity, it is the counterbalancing principle to Chesed. Its main idea can be summed up by the word 'discipline'.

Dion Fortune devotes a great part of her chapter to strictures upon the Christian Faith for its failure to understand, and provide for, a Geburah principle to keep the loving kindness of Chesed in equilibrium. In fact she is criticizing a failure common among those on the fringe of the faith rather than those who hold it in its fulness. The concept of the love of God and the judgement of God as being two sides of a single coin is fundamental to a right understanding of the Christian revelation. Love and judgement (or severity – or as usually rendered, 'wrath') are experienced according to the standpoint of the person experiencing. This accords well with the idea of the two Sephiroth Chesed and Geburah on the pillars. Equilibrium is in the middle and depends upon both. The surgeon and the dentist are 'Geburah figures'. The hand that slaps the spoilt child represents Geburah, but the motive is Chesed! The risen Lord says, 'whom I love, I chasten!' Growth in grace is by love through chastening. There is little in the idea of Geburah to puzzle or disquiet an informed Christian.

Judgement is, as it were, built in to actions and choices. Geburah is the built-in judgement in action. Wars and rumours of wars are Geburah conditions, not in that they are evil – there is nothing 'black' about Geburah – but because they are the inevitable consequences of a succession of unbalanced, wrongheaded and self-glorifying choices. Geburah corrects the vices of Chesed, but to be more precise, the consequences of the vices of Chesed are worked out in Geburah.

The alternative title, 'justice', expresses this principle quite admirably; it is an automatic, cause-and-effect kind of justice. Within the Christian dispensation, the *guilt* of sin is taken away by the Cross of Christ in which the penitent can place his trust. The immediate *effects* have often to be endured with resignation. Thus a brawl which issues in the loss of an eye or a limb may be the subject of forgiveness, but the injury remains. The injury may well be transformed into a means of grace, given penitence and humble acceptance. The Geburah principle is thus enlarged in scope, but it is not only a valid principle, it is a fundamental one.

It may be observed, in any study of social history, that there is a kind of pendulum swinging between the two Sephiroth, Chesed and Geburah. It is a behavioural pendulum. One age is permissive, the next is restrictive, and a great deal of travel between the two extremes may be observed. Man, in this life, is some way from 'middle pillar' stability.

Gareth Knight devotes a considerable proportion of his chapter to the second title, alternative to Geburah. He frankly dislikes the title Pachad – fear. There is, however, some confusion about the nature of the fear. Fear, in current English usage, has come to mean a kind of animal terror. It is manifested at the dentist's front door, in the school playground when bullies are about, and when the possibility arises of battle, murder and sudden death. This is not the fear we are talking about. Fear, in its Biblical context (and this is a Hebrew mystical philosophy that we are dealing with) means 'the Fear of the Lord'. Perhaps a better word would be respect. The fear is the child's reaction to a strict but kindly father. Loving obedience rather than cowed apprehension is what is meant here. God is love and perfect love casts out fear in its morbid manifestation. Fear is better understood as an acknowledgement of utter dependence, morally and metaphysically, upon a loving father ; and as such it is not a bad title for a Sephirah which corrects the Chesed vices of bigotry and hypocrisy.

The vices associated with Geburah are excesses of its nature: cruelty and destruction. Its virtues include courage, and moral courage is much needed in Geburah-like operations. The right arm is its correspondence in microcosm.

Of the tarot, Dion Fortune writes:

'The four fives of the tarot pack are all evil cards, each according to its type. In fact the whole suit of swords, which is under the presidency of Mars, represents contentiousness; for its best aspects are "rest from strife" and "success after struggle", and where a sword card is associated with a Sephirah whose Mundane Chakra is one of the astrological infortunes, the result is disastrous, and we find the Lords of Defeat and Ruin in this suit.' [1]

She concludes her chapter thus: 'When a soul is at that stage of development when the only way it can learn is by experience, Geburah sees that it shall not be disappointed when it goes about looking for trouble. Geburah is the great initiator of the swollen-headed.'[2]

References

1 Fortune, p. 186
2 Fortune, p. 187

Tiphareth

The sixth path is called the mediating intelligence, because in it are multiplied the influxes of the emanations; for it causes that influence to flow into all the reservoirs of the blessings with which they themselves are united.

THE six Sephiroth which centre on Tiphareth are occasionally described by Qabalists as 'archetypal man'. These six constitute the archetypal 'kingdom' which lies behind the kingdom of form in Malkuth. It will be as well to indicate something of the nature of the three Sephiroth that we have not yet encountered. Chesed and Geburah we have studied; Tiphareth, which completes the moral triangle, is the subject of this chapter.

We must take note of the fact that the astral (psychological – or magical) triangle is made up of Netzach – the sphere of Nature forces and elemental contacts; Hod – the sphere of ceremonial magic and occult knowledge, and Yesod – the sphere of what Dion Fortune calls psychism and the etheric double. We are reminded that, in the Qabalistic understanding, the moral triangle has to do with the individuality or 'higher self', and the psychological triangle with the personality or 'lower self'.

Tiphareth is a Sephirah which the Christian will find particularly interesting. It will be very much worth our while to quote Dion Fortune on the function of Tiphareth as the 'Christ-centre'.

'In Tiphareth we find the archetypal ideals brought to a focus and transmuted into archetypal ideas. It is, in fact, the place of incarnation. For this reason it is called the child. And because incarnation of the god-ideal also implies the sacrificial discarnation, to Tiphareth are assigned the mysteries of the crucifixion, and all the sacrificed Gods are placed here when the tree is applied to the pantheons. God the Father is assigned to Kether; but God the Son is assigned to Tiphareth for the reasons given above. Exoteric religion goes no farther up the tree than Tiphareth. It has no understanding of the mysteries of creation as represented by the symbolism of Kether, Chokmah, and Binah; or of the modes of operation of the dark and bright archangels as represented in the symbolism of Geburah and Gedulah; nor of the mysteries of consciousness and the transmutation of force as represented in the invisible Sephirah Daath which has no symbolism.

'In Tiphareth God is made manifest in form and dwells among us, i.e. comes within range of human consciousness. Tiphareth, the Son, "shows us" Kether, the father. In order that form may be stabilized, the component forces out of which it is built must be brought into equilibrium. Therefore do we find the idea of the mediator, or redeemer, inherent in this Sephirah. When the Godhead its very self manifests in form, that form must be perfectly equilibrated. ... Having come through into manifestation on the planes of form in the child aspect of Tiphareth, the incarnated God grows to manhood and becomes the redeemer. In other words, having obtained incarnation by means of matter in a virgin state, i.e. Mary, Marah, the Sea, the Great Mother, Binah, a Supernal, as distinguished from the inferior mother, Malkuth, the developing God-manifestation, is for ever striving to bring the kingdom of the six central Sephiroth into a state of equilibrium. ... The redeemer, then, manifests in Tiphareth, and is for ever striving to redeem his kingdom by returning it to the supernals across the gulf made by the fall, which separated the lower Sephiroth from the higher, and by bringing the diverse forces of the sixfold kingdom into equilibrium. To this end are the incarnated gods sacrificed, dying for the people, in order that the tremendous emotional force set free by this act may compensate the unbalanced force of the kingdom and thus redeem it.'[1]

We may take note of the fact that this is 'redemption by magic'; tremendous emotional force set free is the basis of at least part of the magic-religion of the ancient Celts, whose hilltop mass-hysteria shrines (where the magician sought to focus the raw emotion produced by blood-sacrifice or sex-rituals) may be traced on the map, in triangles and pentangles, by those interested in such matters. Dion Fortune continues:

'It is this sphere on the tree that is called the Christ-centre and it is here that the Christian religion has its focusing-point. The pantheistic faiths, such as the Greek and Egyptian, centre in Yesod; and the *metaphysical faiths*, such as the Buddhist and *Confucian*, aim at Kether. But as all religions worthy of the name have both an esoteric, or mystical, and an exoteric, or pantheistic, aspect, Christianity, although it is essentially a Tiphareth faith, has its mystical aspect centring in Kether, and its magical aspect, as seen in popular continental Catholicism, centring in Yesod. Its evangelical aspect aims at a concentration on Tiphareth as child and sacrificed God, and ignores the aspect of the king in the centre of his kingdom, surrounded by the five holy Sephiroth of manifestation.'[2]

The mixture of the profound and the bizarre in the long quotation from Dion Fortune will provide much food for thought. The insights, many of which are clearly valid, are of course confined within the Qabalistic strait-jacket. Here, as clearly as anywhere, the Christian will perceive the fundamental impossibility – and at the same time the undoubted plausibility – of an attempt to confine the Christian Revelation within a set philosophical framework such as this. He will see, at the same time, how difficult it is for the Qabalist to escape from his system. He will sympathize with the Qabalist's fundamental inability to perceive that only the Christian, standing *outside* the Tree of Life (as, in the Christ, he does) is able to *use* it objectively. The syncretist, be he Western occultist or Eastern Hindu is very genuinely hard put to it to see that the exchange of an all-embracing syncretism for the absolute exclusiveness of Christ and his Church is in fact a *liberation!*

Dion Fortune underlines this for us: 'The different additional titles and symbolism assigned to the various Sephiroth, and especially the God-names thereof, give us a very important key for the unlocking of the mysteries of the Bible, *which is essentially a Qabalistic book* [my italics]. According to the manner in which deity is referred to, we know to what sphere on the tree the particular mode of manifestation should be assigned. All references to the Son always refer to Tiphareth ; all references to the father refer to Kether; all references to the Holy Ghost refer to Yesod; and very deep mysteries are concealed here, for the Holy Ghost is the aspect of the Godhead that is worshipped in the occult lodges; the worship of pantheistic nature-forces and elemental operations take place under the presidency of God the Father; and the regenerative ethical aspect of religion, *which is the exoteric aspect for this epoch* [my italics], is under the presidency of God the Son in Tiphareth.'[6]

There is enough in this last passage to make a patristic scholar cry aloud; and his grief will be hardly lessened by Dion Fortune's next sentence which assures us that the initiate transcends his epoch, and aims at uniting all three modes of adoration in his worship of deity as a trinity in unity. It cannot be stressed enough that, in Hinduism, be it Eastern or Western, Yogic or Qabalistic, there are no formal creeds as Christians understand them. There is merely an underlying philosophy, in both cases monistic, with variations, each Guru playing his own very distinct cadenza.

The 'God-name' attributed to this Sephirah is rendered in translation, 'God made manifest in the sphere of mind.' Tiphareth is as 'high' as the mind can go up the pillar of consciousness. Simple brain-consciousness is confined to Malkuth; psychic consciousness – a far deeper 'awareness' – is the sphere of Yesod, and the 'higher psychism' centres on Tiphareth. This general framework accords well with human experience. To a considerable degree it is supported by certain aspects of psychotherapy, and it is the framework taken for granted in both Yoga and occult meditation. We shall consider these three things in a later section of this book.

The 'spiritual experience' of Tiphareth is the power to enjoy the 'Knowledge and conversation of the Holy Guardian Angel'. This Holy Guardian Angel is not quite the being that might be supposed. It is the 'higher self'. Of the moral triangle, the higher self, which centres on Tiphareth, Dion Fortune writes; 'It is this Second Triad which forms the oversoul, the higher self, the Holy Guardian Angel, the first initiator. It is the voice of this higher self which is so often heard with the inner ear, and not the voice of discarnate entities, or of God Himself, as is thought by those who have had no training in tradition. ... It is the prime characteristic of this higher mode of mentation that it consists neither in voices nor visions, but is pure consciousness; it is an intensification of awareness, and from this quickening of the mind comes a peculiar power of insight and penetration which is of the nature of hyper-developed intuition. The higher consciousness is never psychic, but always intuitive, containing no sensory imagery. It is this absence of sensory imagery which tells the experienced initiate that he is on the level of the higher consciousness.'[4]

Dion Fortune's Christology and Trinitarian theology are bizarre, but in this last paragraph she is on firmer ground.

There are a number of ways advocated by the various schools of occult thought of arriving at this 'knowledge and conversation'. Crowley, in his book *Magick in Theory and Practice*, gives a 'Ritual employed by the beast 666 for the attainment of the knowledge and conversation of his holy guardian angel during the semester of his performance of the operation of the sacred magick of Abramelin the Mage.'[5] The details are repellent.

Unless we are reminded that raw emotion and hysteria are the 'materials' with which the ceremonial magician frequently works, we are likely to find Crowley's ritual not merely repellent, but also utterly meaningless. But it is anything but meaningless. Crowley's intention, firmly monist, was that of self-expansion to the power infinity, and this initiation in which the whole personality is deliberately involved in an ecstatic frenzy, by incantations and auto-eroticism, was but a milestone on the way.

The same underlying philosophy, but with a wholly different 'atmosphere' can be perceived in Mouni Sadhu's book *Concentration*. In the final set of Yogic exercises, 'Crystal-white Pranayama,' he writes, 'and now – *expand* yourself, your "I", your consciousness, or, perhaps, that strange "sight" which can see in all directions simultaneously. Call it what you wish, but expand *this* which is just "you" in *all* dimensions and directions. ... Gradually, like an imaginary luminous blast from the "centre" *explode* into space. First, grow beyond your body, room, house, city, country and planet ... proceed to "go" further and further, beyond galaxies and new universes, always as if from the centre of a sphere in *all* directions to the whole of its ever receding periphery . ... *Go as far as you can* ... only the *expansion*, ever faster and faster. How far will you go? Experience shows that if the expansion which was undoubtedly initiated under your mind's direction at the beginning of the "flight", is pushed ahead to a certain "point" ... the "movement" stops. A man is then bathed in the light of pure, unstained consciousness, and all remembrances of earth and every "outside" thing are effaced. *Then you know.*'[6]

This meditative search for the initiation of Tiphareth will be the subject of considerable study later in this work. The Christian who is called to a contemplative way of prayer will recognize what is being sought here, as well as the limitations imposed by the means employed. But for the time being we must attend to a new, strange study, that of the elementals. Gareth Knight writes:

'There is a great healing power in nature of course, the sphere of the elements, and the four elemental kings, the rulers of the peoples of each element can be assigned to Tiphareth, though the sphere of the elements pertains really to Malkuth. The tradition is quite well known that elementals, being units of life created by the early building powers of the universe and not emanating from the realms of spiritual reality, have only phenomenal and not noumenal existence. Thus when the day of manifestation comes to an end they will become extinct unless in the meantime they have picked up the vibration of spiritual being during the course of it. They can obtain this chance of immortality from any evolution inhabiting the planet whose bodily shell they hold in being and so on earth they rely on contacts with humanity. One only has to take a look round at humanity to be filled with a grave doubt as to their chances. The large proportion of humanity is ignorant of its own spirituality, let alone of the need for mediating this quality. And even where man has achieved high spiritual awareness it has been too often accompanied by a contempt and horror of the physical being. Mediaeval theology branded all elemental beings as devils and in modern times their existence is denied. Thus the adept has always been considered the initiator of the elemental Kingdoms as the only one qualified by reason of spiritual stature and realization so to do. ... When an elemental has attained spiritual awareness it can be said to have Tiphareth consciousness and the elemental kings, those elementals that have attained this state, are also way-showers to them. The elemental kings go by the names of Paralda, for air; Niksa, for water; Ghob, for earth; and Djin, for fire; but a full consideration of the elemental evolution really belongs to Malkuth.'[7]

We shall encounter the idea of elementals in a later section of this book, but they make their debut here.

Knight, noting the fact that the Mundane Chakra of Tiphareth is the Sun, embarks upon a lengthy dissertation on esoteric solar theology, such as we met in the chapter on Chesed. We need not return to it here, other than to note the idea of the 'evolution of God' which is held in certain occult circles.

The three magical images, the majestic king, the child and the sacrificed god have already been dealt with at the beginning of this chapter. They appear to be unrelated at first sight but, as Dion Fortune points out, 'In the light of what we now know concerning Tiphareth, their significance and relationship appears clearly, speaking through the language of symbolism, especially when studied in the light of the life of Jesus Christ the Son.'[8]

Tiphareth is the central Sephirah in more ways than one. It is possible to spend much time considering the very profound symbols and meanings that Qabalists have come to find in it; but we must go on to the Sephiroth that remain, pausing only to take our accustomed note of the tarot.

'The sixes of the tarot suits are also assigned to Tiphareth, and in them the harmonious and balanced nature of this Sephirah shows clearly. The six of wands is the Lord of Victory. The six of cups, the lord of joy. Even the maleficent suit of swords is tuned to harmony in this sphere, and the six of swords is known as the lord of earned success – that is to say, success achieved after struggle. The six of pentacles is material success; in other words, power in equilibrium.'[9]

References

1   Fortune, pp. 190-1
2   Fortune, pp. 191-2
3   Fortune, p. 198
4   Fortune, pp. 196-7
5   Crowley, p. 265 & ff
6   Mouni Sadhu, *Concentration*, p. 189
7   Knight, Vol. i, pp. 189-40
8   Fortune, p. 205
9   Fortune, p. 215

Netzach

The seventh path is called the occult intelligence because it is the refulgent splendour of the intellectual virtues which are perceived by the eyes of the intellect and the contemplations of faith.

THE four lower Sephiroth, in terms of man, the microcosm, represent what Qabalists uderstand as the personality; that part of him which has to do with his present incarnation. It is this personality which, in Qabalistic eyes, is affected by the fall.

Those Qabalists who hold a doctrine of the fall generally confine its effects to the four lower Sephiroth, the 'Christ-centre' of Tiphareth being the place and principle of reconciliation and restoration.

'The great tide of evolving life, which issued as an emanation from Tiphareth, is broken up in the Sephirah Netzach as by a prism into many-rayed manifestation; whence comes the Yetziratic description of this Sephirah as "the refulgent splendour". In Hod these multifarious forces are clothed upon with form; and in Yesod they act as etheric moulds for the final emanations in Malkuth.'[1]

Here we have the idea behind the four lower Sephiroth in a nutshell.

'Netzach, the sphere of Venus, is best understood by contrasting it with Hod, the sphere of Mercury, these two representing force and form on a lower arc, as has already been seen. Netzach represents the instincts and the emotions they give rise to and Hod represents the concrete mind. In the macrocosm they represent two levels of the process of the concretion of force into form. ... In Netzach a particular form of force represents itself as a type of beings, flowing backwards and forwards over the boundaries of manifestation in an exceedingly elusive manner. Such beings have no individualized personalities. ... In Hod, however, individualization into units has taken place and there is continuity of existence. All mind is group-mind in Netzach, but in Hod the human mind has its beginnings. ... Everything that is perceived by the "eyes of the intellect and the contemplations of faith", as the Yetziratic text so graphically puts it, has its metaphysical basis in Chokmah, the supernal Sephirah at the head of the pillar of mercy. But with Netzach a great change comes over our mode of apprehending the different types of existence assigned to each sphere. Hitherto we have perceived by means of intuition;

our apprehensions have been formless, or at least represented by highly abstract symbols; there are no more of these after Tiphareth, but we come to such concrete symbols as the rose, assigned to Venus, for Netzach, and the caduceus, assigned to Mercury, for Hod ... here we have not force, but forces; not life, but lives. Appropriately, therefore, the Order of Angels assigned to Netzach are the Elohim, or gods. The One has been reduced to the Many for the purposes of manifestation in form.' [2]

These 'gods' must be thought of not so much as intelligences as the embodiments of ideas. They are formative influences whereby the creative force expresses itself in nature. In Netzach, the image-making mind of man begins to work on what occultists call the 'astral light', and forms are produced with which the human consciousness can cope.

'It is very important that we should realize that these lower Sephiroth of the plane of illusion are densely populated by thought-forms; that everything which the human imagination has been able to conceive, however dimly, has a form built about it out of the astral light, and that the more the human imagination has dwelt upon it to idealize it, the more definite that form becomes. ... When his mentality was still primitive man worshipped these images, by means of which he represented to himself the great natural forces so all-important to his material well-being, thus establishing a link with them. ... Generations of worship and adoration build a very strong image in the astral light, and when sacrifice is added to worship, the image is brought a step farther down the planes into manifestation and acquires a form in the dense ethers of Yesod, and is a very potent magical object, *capable of independent action* [my italics] when ensouled by the concrete ideas generated in Hod. ... Although the form under which the god is represented is pure imagination, the force associated with it is both real and active. This fact is the key, not only to talismanic magic in its broadest sense, which includes all consecrated objects used in ceremonial and for meditation, but to many things in life that we cannot fail to observe but for which we have no explanation.' [3]

Dion Fortune is quoted at length in most of these chapters because she has a gift of making main points very clearly and briefly. We shall return to the subject of magic in the third section of this book, but here we have an indication of the philosophy behind it, of the very deliberate manufacture of 'gods' in man's own image; the deliberate concretion of 'force' into forms.

The Yetziratic Text speaks of the 'refulgent splendour of the intellectual virtues'. Gareth Knight considers that this is a misleading rendering and prefers 'the refulgent splendour of the psyche', which, he says, 'is really the force of the creative imagination, and so Netzach is the sphere whence emanates the inspiration not only of the artist but of all who work creatively. It is a Sephirah of perfect balance of force and form, though anteceding the concretion of mental forms in Hod, and the awareness of the perfect balance produces ecstasy, joy, delight and fulfilment or, in other words, the spiritual experience of the vision of beauty triumphant. The result of approaches to this perfection of balance manifests ultimately not only in great works of art but also in the beauty of well designed tools, machinery, scientific instruments and so on, for perfection of precision in use gives beauty of form. ... There is an alliance between art and invention – as has been demonstrated by the genius of Leonardo da Vinci – and this is because both emanate from the "psychic refulgence" of Netzach, the creative imagination.'

'Anyone,' he goes on to say, 'who has ever attempted creative work, will know the feeling of vast inertia that has to be overcome. ... However, this inertia is overcome, and the means of its overcoming is the flaming creative energy of Netzach, for Netzach is an active Sephirah, being assigned to the element of fire as is its higher diagonal opposite, Geburah, and Geburah's higher diagonal opposite, Chokmah.'[4]

One of the principal ideas embodied in Netzach is the idea of polarity. Knight spends a considerable time discussing this principle as he finds it manifested in various human relationships. David and Jonathan are given as examples of the principle as manifested in friendships between persons of the same sex. As between persons of opposite sex, Knight and Fortune take somewhat differing views. Knight stresses the fact that responsible occultism is on the side of 'old-fashioned morality', for good reasons. Fortune prefers to make much of the Aphrodite cult and the place of the Greek hetaera whose function was 'to minister to the intellect of her clients as well as their appetites; she was a hostess as well as a mistress'.[6]

Knight's work has the title, *A Practical Guide to Qabalistic Symbolism*, and he is less concerned with classical niceties as with the practical workings-out of Qabalism in every-day life in this century. Polarity is also manifested between 'force and form' proceeding from the same source, as between brother and sister, between whom a deep psychological rapport may often be found. Polarity between 'higher and lower' such as father and son; polarity between teacher and pupil, between the one and the many in group relationships – these and many other manifestations of the principle are listed by Knight, who makes mention of a number of mythological and literary 'initiatory types'.

There is a most striking correspondence in thought between the modern occultist's valid preoccupations with polarity, as he finds this under the heading of Netzach, and the five basic human relationships taught by Confucius as being the keys to world harmony. These five are ruler and subject; father and son; husband and wife; elder brother and younger, and friend and friend. Given a right 'polarity' in all these, says Confucius, then the world will be in harmony. Alas! The roots of disharmony go deeper than this, but the insight, as far as it goes, is both profound and valid. It is found again in Netzach.

We have already touched upon the subject of magic. The two Sephiroth, Netzach and Hod, are the spheres of magic; they cannot be considered in isolation. 'The functions of Netzach are implicit in Hod because Netzach emanates Hod, and the powers developed by evolution in the sphere of Netzach are the basis of the capacities of Hod [the sphere of ceremonial magic]. Consequently all magical operations of the sphere of Hod work upon a basis of the tenuous life-forms of Netzach; and because the human intellect works up from sphere to sphere, a good deal of the powers of Hod have been carried over into Netzach by initiated souls going on ahead of evolution. … All rites which have rhythm and movement and colour in them are a working in the sphere of Netzach. And as Hod, the sphere of magical workings, draws its force from Netzach, it follows that any magical operation of the sphere of Hod must have a Netzach element in it if it is to be ensouled effectually; and in order to provide a basis of manifestation, *etheric substance has to be provided by some form of sacrifice* [my italics], even if it be only the burning of incense.' 6

In terms of man, the microcosm, Netzach is the artist in us, Hod the scientist, says Dion Fortune. There are, she claims, three types of people who – as she puts it – 'pass within the veil'. These are the mystic, the psychic and the occultist. 'The mystic aspires to union with God, and achieves his end by putting aside all that is not of God in his life. The psychic is a receiver of subtle vibrations, but not a transmitter. The occultist must needs be to some extent at least a receiver, but his primary aim is to be able to control and direct in the invisible kingdoms in the same way that the man of science has learned to control and direct in the kingdom of nature.' 7

This is an important observation; we shall return to it at a later stage in this work. Meanwhile, Dion Fortune complains that 'it is because most people who go in for occultism work up the central pillar only, which is the Pillar of Consciousness, and pay no attention to the side pillars, which are the Pillars of Function, that such negligible results are obtained from initiation. The blind are leading the blind, and the average would-be initiator in modern occult fraternities, who is usually more of a mystic than an occultist, does not realise that he has got to initiate subconsciousness as well as consciousness, and illuminate the instincts as well as the reason.'[8]

Finally, let us consider the tarot. 'Lucky in love, unlucky at cards,' quotes Dion Fortune, and continues,

'Venus is a disturbing influence in world affairs. She distracts from the serious business of life. ... The Qabalistic name of the seven of pentacles is "success unfulfilled", and we only have to look at the lives of Cleopatra, Guinevere, Iseult, Héloïse, to realize that Venus upon the physical plane has for her motto, "all for love, and the world well lost". The suite of swords is assigned to the astral plane. The secret title of the seven of swords is "Unstable Effort". How well does this express the action of Venus in the sphere of the emotions, with its short-lived intensity. The secret title of the seven of cups is "illusory success". This card represents the working of Venus in the sphere of mind, where her influence is by no means conducive to clear-sightedness. We believe what we want to believe when we are under the influence of Venus. Upon this plane her motto might well be "love is blind". Only in the sphere of the spirit does Venus come into her own. Here her card, the seven of wands, is called "valour", which well describes the dynamic and vitalizing influence she exerts when her spiritual significance is understood and employed.'[9]

References

1   Fortune, pp. 217-18
2   Fortune, pp. 221-5
3   Fortune, pp. 225-5
4   Knight, pp. 151-2
5   Fortune, p. 228
6   Fortune, pp. 225-6
7   Fortune, pp. 255-4
8   Fortune, p. 251
9   Fortune, pp. 256-7

Hod

The eighth path is called the absolute or perfect intelligence because it is the mean of the primordial, which has no root by which it can cleave or rest, save in the hidden place of Gedulah, from which emanates its proper essence.

IN treating of Netzach, we have already said much concerning Hod. 'Hod: says Gareth Knight, 'is primarily the Sephirah of the forms of the concrete mind and intellect, and as form was first formed in Chesed or Gedulah, which is its diagonal opposite, the relationship between these two Sephiroth is stressed in the Yetziratic Text. It will be seen that Chesed is also a diagonal opposite of Binah, where the idea of form is first conceived and so these three Sephiroth are linked in this way, being regarded as under the presidency of water just as Chokmah, Geburah and Netzach are referred to fire and the line of central Sephiroth to air.'[1]

The symbols and images and elements interwoven into the Tree of Life may be seen to be arranged as a very tidy and all-embracing system. Here lies the source of much of its appeal to Qabalists, and also much of its intrinsic value.

We encountered the idea of magic and some of the philosophy behind it in the previous chapter. Hod is the sphere of ceremonial magic and we can continue our investigations with Dion Fortune as our teacher. 'For the full understanding of the philosophy of magic,' she writes, 'we must remember that single Sephiroth are never functional; for function one must have the pair of opposites in balanced equilibrium, resulting in an equilibriated third which is functional. ... The functioning triangle of the lower triad consists of Hod, Netzach, and Yesod. Hod and Netzach, as we have noted before, are respectively form and force on the astral plane. Yesod is the basis of etheric substance, Akasha, or the astral light, as it is variously called. Hod is especially the sphere of magic, because it is the sphere of the formulation of forms, and is therefore the sphere in which the magician actually works, for it is his mind that formulates the forms, and his will that makes the link with the natural forces of the sphere of Netzach that ensoul them. ... The power of the will projects the magician out of Hod, but only the power of sympathy can take him into Netzach. A cold-blooded person of dominating will can no more be an adept working with power than can a fluidically sympathetic person of pure emotion. The power of the concentrated will is necessary to enable the magician to gather himself together for his work, but the power of imaginative sympathy is essential to enable him to make his contacts. For it is only through our power to enter imaginatively into the life of types of existence different to our own that we can pick up our contacts with the forces of nature. To attempt to dominate them by pure will, cursing them by the Mighty Names of God if they resist, is pure sorcery.'[2]

Dion Fortune, a magician of renown among her fellows, goes on to make it plain that advancement along the magical path is dependent upon the make-up of the intending magician's nature. Concerning initiation, an important idea to the occultist, but a term missing, very largely, from the Christian vocabulary, she says: 'We can only operate in a sphere after we have received the initiation of that sphere, which, in the language of the mysteries, confers its powers. In the technical working of the mysteries these initiations are conferred on the physical plane by means of ceremonial, which may be effectual, or may not. The gist of the matter lies in the fact that one cannot waken into activity what is not already latent. Life is the real initiator. ... Be it well noted that it is only in proportion as our capacities for reaction are lifted out of the sphere of emotional reflexes and brought under rational control that we can make of them magical powers.'[3]

'The Archangel of Hod is Michael, the great guardian who holds at bay the forces of the underworld: writes Gareth Knight. 'In magical working he is assigned to the South, the fire Quarter ... The element of fire is that element which transmutes forms to a higher level and so is associated with Michael by reason of the fact that he deals similarly with unregenerate forms and forces.'[4]

Knight finds it interesting that the Church has venerated Michael as protector and guardian. He is of course the 'guardian angel' of Israel (Daniel xii. 1, and elsewhere). 'There must be hundreds of places dedicated to St Michael and they are usually sites of pagan worship and thus places frequented, according to mediaeval Christian belief, by devils.'[5] Knight refers to St Michael's Mount off Cornwall, Mont St Michel off Brittany, and also the tower on Glastonbury Tor. His observations are shrewd, because, particularly in Celtic parts, this is certainly very often true. Not a few prominent hills which, in Druid times, were worship sites in the great Celtic scheme of triangles and pentangles on the map, with points and intersections as sites for magic worship, have, on or nearby, a church or chapel (ruined or otherwise) dedicated to St Michael, and Llanvihangel (Church of the Angel) is a common Welsh place name on Ordnance

Survey maps. He observes, less shrewdly, that 'the differences between pagan and Christian worship of God are really quite superficial. Basically it is one worship and one God'.[6] The Christian, while acknowledging the truth that is contained in the statement, would be slow to agree with it! It would be interesting to investigate the extent to which the concepts of 'Michael', magical and biblical, have become interwoven over the centuries.

Mercury is the Mundane Chakra of Hod. It is closely connected, in esoteric thought, with both Venus and Earth and has much to do with the psychic levels of the abstract mind, according to this same tradition. The mysteries of Hermes Trismegistus (Mercurius Termaximus, or, in the Egyptian, Thoth-Tehuti) who is a kind of archetypal leader and teacher of mankind, may be considered under Hod. He has given his name to a complete occult tradition – the Hermetic Ray. We have encountered Hermes, briefly, in the first of the introductory essays to this work. 'According to Clement of Alexandria the whole of Egyptian religous philosophy was contained in the Books of Thoth. Thoth, the Lord of Books and of Learning, was regarded as the inspirer of all sacred writings and the teacher of all religion and philosophy ... Thoth was the president of all priestly discipline and every Egyptian priest was held to be a priest of Thoth over and above his other priestly functions because Thoth was the archetypal priest or hierophant – the oversoul of all priests.'[7] Knight makes frequent mention of our Lord as 'key figure of devotional mysticism' as opposed to Orpheus – key figure of nature mysticism – and Hermes (Thoth) – key figure of magic and occult philosophy. Our Lord cannot be 'kept out', but not for the reasons given. The Christian will have recognized already that Hermes (Thoth) is a shadow, a type which our Lord fulfilled.

The tarot, with which we have been keeping in touch as we go through the Tree of Life, is occasionally called the Book of Thoth. Knight writes: 'The origin of the tarot cards is shrouded in obscurity, being placed by some authorities as far back as the Egyptian mysteries and by others as late as the sixteenth century. *However, this type of scholastic research matters nothing for their true origin comes from the inner planes* [my italics] and their authority derives not from the date of their physical inception but from their use as a practical system here and now.'[8]

Dion Fortune, our guide in these matters, tells us that, in respect of Hod, 'The concept of inhibited reaction and satisfaction foregone is expressed in the title of the eight of cups of the tarot pack, whose secret name is "abandoned success" ... The same concept reappears in the secret title of the eight of swords, which is "the lord of shortened force". We get a clear image in these words of the checking, or slowing down, of dynamic power in order that it may be brought under control. In the eight of pentacles, which represents the nature of Hod manifesting on the material plane, we have the lord of prudence – again a checking and inhibiting influence. But all these three negative, inhibiting cards are summed up under the presidency of the eight of wands, which represents the action of the sphere of Hod on the spiritual plane, and this card is called the Lord of Swiftness.'[8]

References

1 Knight, p. 164
2 Fortune, pp. 244-5
3 Fortune, pp. 245-6
4 Knight, p. 167
5 Knight, p. 168
6 Knight, p. 168
7 Knight, p. 170
8 Knight, p. 171
9 Fortune, p. 247

Yesod

The ninth path is called the pure intelligence because it purifies the emanations. It proves and corrects the designing of their representations, and disposes the unity with which they are designed without diminution or division.

WE are approaching the end of our survey of what is known as the objective Qabalah, the ten Sephiroth on the Tree of Life. In the Qabalistic understanding, the whole of that which the Christian would call creation has emanated from the first 'nothingness concreting a centre' of Kether, through the archetypal ideas of force and form in Chokmah and Binah, down, back and forth from one side of the tree to the other, following the Sephiroth in their order, until the penultimate Sephirah is arrived at; Yesod, the sphere of the Machinery of the Universe.

'Yesod is the sphere of that peculiar substance, partaking of the nature of both mind and matter, which is called the Aether of the Wise, the Akasha, or the Astral Light, according to the terminology that is being used,' says Dion Fortune. 'It is not the same as the ether of the physicists which is the fire element of the sphere of Malkuth; but is to that ether what that ether is to dense matter; it is, in fact, the basis of the phenomena which the physicist attributes to his empirical ether. The Aether of the Wise might, in fact, be called the root of the ether of physics.'[1]

The terminology is not particularly helpful at this point and we are on more familiar ground with Knight. Dion Fortune and Gareth Knight belong to different generations. Their approaches to their subject are subtly different in a number of ways. Fortune was a renowned magician and although her approach is by no means as magically orientated as the approach of some authorities, it is noticeably more so than that of Gareth Knight whose concerns are essentially practical and meditational; the second of his two volumes is entirely devoted to the meditational aspect of the Tree of Life; 'path-working', or as it is sometimes described, the subjective Qabalah. His terminology is usually more 'up-to-date' in style.

Yesod, in his view, is the powerhouse of the machinery of the physical world and holds together the framework in which the particles of dense matter are enmeshed. The Thomist concepts of Form and Matter are echoed in Knight.

'The study of the etheric is a vast one, for it is coextensive with the whole range of the physical sciences but its effect in the physical world can be regarded approximately as vitality. It is an energy of integration which co-ordinates the physical molecules, cells and so on into a definite organism, and so without it our physical bodies would be nothing but collections of independent cells. It is not a product of physical life, for Yesod is nearer the source of things than Malkuth, but living creatures, plants and even minerals are its products. … It is the controlling agent in the chemico-physiological changes of protoplasm and shows its presence by the power of organisms to respond to stimuli, and is thus the basis behind those fibrous cells which constitute the nerves and give the power to feel pleasure and pain. It is held by esoteric science that *it is the etheric vehicle and not the physical body which has the power to feel* [my italics], and this is the principle behind certain anaesthetics; they drive the etheric double out of the physical body as occurs in sleep, deep trance and finally at death. The physical body is the receiver of physical sense impressions only and has no acute sensory awareness except as vague, dull, diffused feelings such as general fatigue. The formation of a nervous system is caused by an admixture of astral with etheric forces and so there is only rudimentary nervous structure in plants and none at all in minerals. All however, have their structure built and held by the etheric web or network, thus it is the foundation of physical existence, and "the foundation" is the Title of Yesod.'[2]

This passage is of very great importance indeed if we are to begin to understand the principles and philosophy behind the magico-meditation that will confront us in the next section of the book. Knight goes on to maintain that Yesod may be said to hold the image of everything that exists in the physical world, and is thus also titled the 'treasure-house of images'.

Having clarified Fortune by reference to Knight, we may now return to Fortune. 'The material universe is an insoluble riddle to the materialist,' she claims, 'because he insists on trying to explain it in terms of his own plane. This is a thing that can never be done in any sphere of thought. Nothing can ever be explained in terms of itself, but only by being resumed in a greater whole. … Yesod, then, must be conceived of as the receptacle of the emanations of all the other Sephiroth, as taught by the Qabalists, and as the Immediate and only transmitter of these emanations to Malkuth, the physical plane.'[3]

Yesod is the penultimate Sephirah, there remains the tenth Sephirah, Malkuth, the 'kingdom', which in the diagram of the tree hangs like a pendant beneath the astral (or psychological) triangle, whose downward-pointing apex is Yesod. Malkuth is the physical world, the final, the most concrete principle of manifestation. The Qabalist's view of things is nothing if not orderly.

'The only approach to Malkuth is through Yesod and the approach to Yesod is through Hod, where the "representations" are "designed". Let us once and for all disabuse our minds of the idea that spirit can work directly upon matter; it never does so. Spirit works through mind, and mind works through the Aether; and the Aether, which is the framework of matter and the vehicle of the life-forces, can be manipulated within the limits of its nature, which are by no means inconsiderable. *All miraculous and supernatural happenings, therefore, are brought about by the manipulation of the natural qualities of the aether, and if we understood the nature of the aether, we should understand the rationale of their production* [my italics]. We should no longer attribute them to the direct intervention of God, or to the activities of the spirits of the departed, than we attribute nowadays the phenomena of combustion to the activities of phlogiston ... the day will come when men will look upon psychic phenomena and "spiritual" healing as we look upon phlogiston.' [4]

Yesod is the all-important sphere for magic which is designed to take effect In the physical world, just as, according to Fortune, Tiphareth is the functional sphere of mysticism, with its transcendent contacts with the supernal. Knight dwells at great length (as does Fortune) upon the moon-symbolism of Yesod. He mentions the symbols of the sandals and the perfumes as magical implements, the one enabling us to 'walk with ease' on the foundations of the various psychic levels, the other being strongly evocative and a great aid to *changes in consciousness*, which by definition is of the very essence of magic. Knight spends some time discussing the moon-figures of the Old Testament, from Moses on Sinai – the moon-mountain, the mountain of vision – through a number of speculative interpretations of institutions and phenomena, to the moon-symbolism of the building of the Temple. He gives us, in addition, a most interesting Qabalistic interpretation of the Ten Commandments!

1. *Thou shalt have no other gods before me* refers to the unity of Kether.
2. *Thou shalt not take unto thee any graven image* refers to the formless devotion of Chokmah where the only image is the vision of God face to face.
3. *Thou shalt not take the name of the Lord thy God in vain* has reference to the virtue of silence in Binah, the root of faith.
4. *Remember the Sabbath day, to keep it holy. Six days shalt thou labour, etc.*

Six is the number of Tiphareth and the observance of the Sabbath or seventh day has reference to the devotion to the Great Work and the vision of the harmony of things in Tiphareth.

5. *Honour thy father and thy mother* refers to Chesed whose virtue is obedience.

6. *Thou shalt not kill* relates to Geburah.

7. *Thou shalt not commit adultery* although superficially it may seem to refer to the vice of Netzach really applies to Yesod, the Sephirah of purification – the pure intelligence.

8. *Thou shalt not steal* is an exhortation to the virtue of Netzach, unselfishness, and the firmness and valour of this Sephirah. Theft is an underhand weakness and a sheer abuse of all principles of polarity, for theft can apply to other levels beside the physical.

9. *Thou shalt not bear false witness* relates to Hod. The Qliphothic (demonic) aspect of Hod is referred to as 'the false accuser' and in the Greek pantheon the averse side of Hermes was considered to be the patron of thieves.

10. *Thou shalt not covet thy neighbour's house ... nor anything that is thy neighbour's* refers to the vice of Malkuth – avarice. [5]

These interesting correspondences are an instance of the Qabalist's zeal to claim the Bible as a Qabalistic book. (Knight does not labour that point in this instance.) The correspondences between the Old Testament and Qabalistic terms and thought-forms need not surprise us in the least. In the first place, the Jews of the Christian era evolved the Qabalah out of a continuing Old Testament tradition, as the second of the introductory essays indicates, and in the second place the Qabalah is a very remarkable and all-embracing pattern of symbolisms and archetypes. Its value lies in this very fact; it is a key which, in thoughtful hands, can unlock a great many doors which are usually closed to man's understanding. It is worth saying, once again, that if a key is to open a door it must *be held in the hand.* The Qabalist, possessed of great insights though he may be, is too mixed up *within* the key to use it as objectively as it might be used.

The use of symbolism, in the Qabalah, is a very exact and most disciplined business. It should not be imagined that vagueness has any part in occult proceedings. Every symbol has its place and none must be out of place. Meditational discipline is strict; the occultist is using powerful tools when he meditates upon symbols. By their means – and there is no other means – he is probing the unconscious in his search for reality. He must keep his tools under very firm control. 'One needs an experienced magical method of mentation before dabbling with certain occult matters for the true interpretation of much magical lore depends on analogy, allegory and symbol rather than straightforward logic. In practice this unfortunately works out in the fact that the scientifically minded person considers the occultist to be completely devoid of any powers of logic of sensible reasoning. However occultism is in reality a very exact science – it must be or the practical operator is soon in trouble, and the training of an adept is every bit as rigorous and lengthy as an advanced graduate of one of the sciences. *It is to be hoped that in the future the two methods of mind-working and research will coalesce as indeed they seem to be doing through the field of modern psychiatry* [my italics] and the increasing interest in symbolism and myth.'[6]

This hope will be echoed when we come to study 'magical psychiatry' later in this work, and also when we consider present-day psycho-analytical approaches to various problems.

Not the least among the many symbol-systems tied up with the Qabalah is the tarot, odd though it often seems. It is in fact a very profound system, and a tarot 'divination' is, as Knight makes clear, essentially a way of *training the intuition*. The tarot is not in itself mere mumbo-jumbo – although doubtless it is reduced to that often enough – it is a symbolic training-aid for the intuitive powers of the mind, and a stimulus for them to work from. Having said this, let us be instructed in the tarot symbolism for Yesod.

'In the four tarot cards assigned to this Sephirah how clearly do we see the workings of the etheric magnetism appearing. There is great strength when we are on the earth-contacts and blessed of Pan; there is also material happiness; in fact, without the blessing of Pan there can be no material happiness because there is no peace of the nerves. On its negative side, however, are to be found the depths of despair and cruelty; but with the earth-contacts firm under our feet there comes material gain because we are adequate to deal with the material plane.'[7]

References

1   Fortune, p. 263
2   Knight, pp. 175-6
3   Fortune, p. 264
4   Fortune, p. 266
5   Knight, pp. 185-6
6   Knight, pp. 187-8
7   Fortune, p. 264

Malkuth

The tenth path is called the resplendent intelligence because it is exalted above every head and sits upon the throne of Binah. It illuminates the splendours of all the Lights, and causes an influence to emanate from the prince of countenances, the angel of Kether.

WE have come to the tenth, the final Sephirah, called the kingdom, and equated by those occultists who hold to the Qabalah as their basis of philosophy and belief with material creation. Malkuth is, in a sense, different from the other Sephiroth. It is not specifically aligned with any of the four elements, but is, as it were, divided between them.

'Malkuth is said to be the sphere of earth; but we must not make the mistake of thinking that the Qabalists meant by Malkuth only the terrestrial sphere. They meant also the earth-soul – that is to say, the subtle, psychic aspect of matter; the underlying noumenon of the physical plane which gives rise to all physical phenomena. Likewise with the four elements. These are not earth, air, fire and water as known to the physicists, *but are the four conditions in which energy can exist* [my italics]. The esotericist distinguishes these from their mundane counterparts by referring to them as the air of the wise, or the earth of the wise, as the case may be. That is to say, the element of air or of earth as it is known to the initiate.

'The physicist recognizes the existence of matter in three states. Firstly, as solid, wherein the particles of which it is composed adhere firmly to each other; secondly, liquid, in which the particles move freely over each other; thirdly, gaseous, in which the particles all try to get as far away from each other as possible, or in other words to diffuse. These three modes of matter correspond to the three elements of earth, water, and air, and electrical phenomena corresponds to the element of fire. ...The esotericist sees in Malkuth the end-result of all operations; not until the pairs of opposites have achieved the settled equilibrium which gives the state of earth, or coherence, can they be said to have completed any given cycle of experience.'[1]

No Sephirah can be considered in isolation; Malkuth, which seems, alone of the ten, to be isolated, is meaningless without reference to Yesod, as we have already perceived in our survey of the latter. Yesod is form-giving.

Malkuth represents the 'stuff' in which the form is at last embodied. Matter is inanimate unless Yesod 'ensouls' it. But it should not be thought that Qabalists consider Malkuth to be the ultimate in unspirituality. Malkuth, the kingdom is equally 'holy' with Kether the Crown. Knight would use the words 'equally divine' because this is an emanationist and Monist philosophy. Malkuth can say of itself, 'there is nothing of me which is not of the gods'.

> 'The Yetziratic Text of the Sephirah Malkuth shows the importance of the physical world in the Divine scheme of things. "The tenth path is called the resplendent intelligence because it is exalted above every head and sits upon the throne of Binah." The reference to Binah shows that Malkuth is the supreme manifestation of the form which was first conceived as a possibility in the Supernal World of Binah. It is thus "exalted above every head" for Malkuth is the end result of the divine impulse into manifestation – the spiritual pattern made physically manifest.'[2]

The Qabalist is no Manichee; matter is holy because it is the expression of the divine intention. This much at least the Qabalist shares with the Christian, and it is a great deal. There are echoes here of the great physicist Eddington, who said, somewhere in his writings, 'What physics ultimately finds in the atom, or indeed in any other entity studied by physical means is *the structure of a set of operations.*'[3] He might have said, with Knight, 'the spiritual pattern made physically manifest'.

Pursuing this line of thought, Dion Fortune comments that exoteric science deals with the problem by refining its concept of matter until there is no substance left. The esotericist approaches the problem from the opposite direction. Mind and matter are 'two sides of the same coin, but ... there comes a point in one's investigation when it is profitable to change over one's terminology, and talk of forces and forms in terms of psychology, as if they were conscious and purposive. This ... enables us to deal with the phenomena we encounter much better than we can do if we limit ourselves to terms only applicable to inanimate matter and blind, undirected force. ... It is for this reason that the esotericist personifies the subtler forces and calls them intelligences. He then proceeds to deal with them as if they were intelligent, and he finds that there is a subtle side of his own nature and consciousness which responds to them, and to which, he fondly believes, they respond. At any rate, whether the response is mutual or not, his powers of dealing with them are, by this means, greatly extended beyond those which he possesses when he regards them as "a fortuitous concourse of unrelated incidents".'[4]

We have come down the tree in our survey. This is the sensible way to study the ten Sephiroth, the objective Qabalah. Malkuth is the nadir of evolution, the marker-buoy round which we turn. In an examination of the subjective Qabalah, we should have to start from Malkuth and work back, but in a rather different way, as we shall see shortly. Knight writes,

> 'The various titles of Malkuth which refer to it as a gate show that the physical world is a definite stage in spiritual development or a thing which one must *go through*. The gate of death and the gate of the shadow of death refer to the great boundaries of Malkuth as far as man's physical existence is concerned – birth and death. By birth we come into the world and by death we go out of it. Birth and death however are two sides of the same coin, for when one dies physically one is born into the higher worlds, and when one is born physically, from the point of view of the higher worlds one is dead.'[5]

Malkuth is the gate of tears because of its connection with Binah, where is experienced the vision of sorrow.

Knight's second volume is concerned very largely with the subjective Qabalah, in other words the twenty-two paths that run between the ten Sephiroth. These are followed, triad by triad, from Malkuth to Kether. They are primarily paths of meditation to be followed by man, the microcosm, in his great work of expanding himself to the power infinity. These terms are repugnant to the Christian, but they sound less objectionable when they are changed into Hindu terms. The task of the individual, by means of his yoga, is to finally unite the Atman (individual soul) with the Brahman (world-soul, *solar logos*, or what you will) in a union which absolves him from the sorrow of reincarnation. His karma must be spotless. The great work is not only meritorious, it is what he is for; he must strive to be so truly a yogi that when he departs this life he does not enter it again.

Not for nothing is Qabalistic occultism called 'the Yoga of the West'. As Dion Fortune writes, 'In initiation upon the Western path ... the grades of the lesser mysteries go straight up the central pillar to Tiphareth, and do not follow the line of the lightning flash [the lightning flash is the zig-zag order of manifestation from Kether to Malkuth]. In Tiphareth the initiate takes the first grade of adepthood, and from there returns if he so desires, to learn the technique of the magician relative to the personality of the tree, that is to say the macrocosmic unit of incarnation. If he does not desire this, but wishes to become free from the wheel of birth and death, he proceeds up the central pillar, which is also called by the Qabalists the path of the arrow, and passes over the Abyss into Kether. He who enters this light cometh not forth again.'[6]

There is a great deal written in Dion Fortune's chapter on Malkuth concerning the charging of talismans and the affairs of magic in the sphere of Malkuth. Evocation, mediumship and magical weapons are touched upon. In the end, she writes, 'The best magical weapon is the magus himself, and all other contrivances are but a means to an end, the end being that exaltation and concentration of consciousness which makes a magus of an ordinary man. "Know ye not that ye are the temple of the living God?" said a great one. If we know how to use the symbolic furniture of this living temple, we have the keys of heaven in our hands.'[7]

There is a great wealth of symbolism described in both the authoritative books that we have taken as our guide through these last twelve chapters. It has been necessary to cut the available material down to the minimum which will convey the essentials of the Tree of Life as Qabalists understand it. The tables of symbols and titles which form an appendix to this part of the work will be found to contain a very great deal of food for thought and meditation. Before we conclude this part of the book, with a brief summary of interim conclusions about the Qabalah as we have found it, let us turn once more to the tarot.

'In the sphere of Malkuth are worked all divinations. Now the object of any method of divination is to find a set of things on the physical plane which correspond accurately and comprehensively to the invisible forces in the same way that the movements of the hands of a clock correspond to the passage of time … It is of little use to go into a shop and buy a pack of tarot cards unless there is the knowledge necessary to build up the astral correspondences to each card. This takes time, as there are seventy-two cards to work with. Once it is done, however, the operator can take the cards into his hands with a considerable degree of confidence that his subconscious mind whatever that may be, will all unwittingly deal the cards that refer to the matter in question.'[8]

Of the cards assigned to Malkuth, she writes, 'The four tarot cards yield curious results when subjected to meditation in the light of what we know about Malkuth. The ten of wands is called the Lord of Oppression; the ten of cups, the Lord of Perfected Success; the ten of swords, the Lord of Ruin; and the ten of pentacles, the Lord of Wealth.' She contrasts the alternate good-bad significance and points out that the most spiritual in nature are outwardly corrosive, and the most material are beneficial on the physical plane.

'These four cards, then, give a very true insight into the nature of the operation of forces in Malkuth, and when they turn up in a divination, one always prepares for the outward gold to turn to corrosion, and the outward corrosion to turn to gold sooner or later, and one takes in or spreads one's sails accordingly.'[9]

References

1   Fortune, pp. 266-7
2   Knight, p. 191
3   F. G. Happold, *Religious Faith and Twentieth Century Man*, p. 61
4   Fortune, p. 270
5   Knight, p. 192
6   Fortune, pp. 268-9
7   Fortune, p. 281
8   Fortune, p. 288
9   Fortune, pp. 294-6

Some Conclusions

IT is time to try to arrive at some conclusions about the Qabalah as it has revealed itself to us. Some kind of assessment, an interim judgement must be made. It is not by any means the purpose of this book to seek a reconciliation between what the last twelve chapters have presented to us and orthodox Christian belief. But it is not the purpose of this book to debunk or to condemn either; if there had not existed, from the outset, a conviction that this whole construction had an intrinsic value in its own right, then there would have been small point in setting pen to paper. We must ask some serious questions about the Qabalah, as Gentile occultists use it, and we shall ask our questions about the Qabalah as they themselves describe it. It would have been a fairly simple matter to have begun the foregoing chapters with the words, 'Qabalists believe that ...' and to have embarked upon a description from the outside. But it would have been from the outside only; it is not possible for a Christian to fully enter a pre-Christian religious philosophy and write from within as a believer in all that he is writing about. Dion Fortune and Gareth Knight both believed in what they wrote, and they wrote from the inside. They have therefore been our guides and it is their Qabalah which must provoke our questions.

The first question that must be asked is obvious: How true is the occult, Gentile Qabalah to the Jewish Qabalistic tradition?

If we go back to the second of the introductory essays and refresh our memories, we find at once that we seem to be in another world altogether. The origins of the Qabalah lie within the alphabetical mysticism of early Judaism. The *Sepher Yetzirah*, holy writ to our latter-day Qabalists, speaks of a wholly different construction from that with which we have been dealing. It is a brief, obscure speculation upon the ten numbers and the twenty-two letters of the Hebrew alphabet. These are *the means of conscious expression*. Without them no rational thought can be expressed. They are thus creative principles, especially to the Jews to whom Hebrew was the 'language of heaven'. God spoke Hebrew!

We must not laugh at the idea of a 'divine language'; the inertia of the churches in this respect has been remarkable. The Roman Church is only now struggling free of Latin – gibberish to nearly all her members;

the Russian Church still uses Old Slavonic at times; the Malankarese of Malabar pray partly in Syrian, the Ethiopians in Geez, and the Anglicans in late Middle English! The creative principles, the 'thirty-two paths' of the *Sepher Yetzirah*, have been the subject of unbridled speculation in spite of the warning against speculation: 'close your mouth lest it speak and your heart lest it think'. The Yetziratic Text, from which our chapter-heading quotations have come, is not less than one thousand years younger than the book of which it is an appendix! God spoke and creation 'was so'. This is the real understanding behind the *Sepher Yetzirah;* the rest is speculation.

Abulafia used the *Sepher Yetzirah* as the basis of his system of ecstaticism, using the device of combining and permutating letters in order to arrive at the 'great name of God' and enter an ecstatic state. Zen Buddhists speak of Satori; Hindus of Samahdi; the end-product is one and the same. Contemporary with Abulafia, we find the Spanish Jews evolving the Qabalah as we begin to recognize it on another line of thought altogether.

The Sephiroth of the *Zohar* add up to the 'one great name of God'. Their titles are divine attributes, and if St Paul had had the diagrammatic turn of mind of his later countrymen, he too might perhaps have drawn a pattern of ten circles and named them love, joy, peace, long-suffering, gentleness, goodness, faith, meekness, temperance, with as his 'Malkuth' the bride of Christ, the Church. Such a tree of life would not be difficult to draw. God 'emanates' his attributes to the human understanding.

But what about Malkuth? It is the difference between the Malkuths, Jewish and Gentile, that is the most striking. To the occultist, Malkuth is the physical world. To the Jew it is more subtle than this, *it is the archetype of Israel, the people of God.* It is the Shekhinah, the Bride of Yahweh, separated from grace by the fall. Our 'Pauline Qabalah' is very much nearer to the spirit of the *Zohar* than the speculative construction we have been studying.

Isaac Luria, the prophet of Messianic Qabalism, is perhaps the link between the Qabalah of the Zohar and that of the occultists. Luria introduced the idea of the 'four worlds' and was forced to invent a doctrine of 'Tsimtsum' or 'divine withdrawal' to counteract the intrinsic Pantheism of the Qabalah as it developed. (The doctine of Tsimtsum is, curiously enough, echoed in some of the speculations of the 'Death of God' theologian, T.J.J. Altizer!) Pantheism (or monism) is abhorrent to the Jew, and throughout its Jewish history, anti-pantheist devices have had to be applied to the Qabalah to safeguard the strongly transcendent doctrine of God that is such a feature of Judaism. The Gentile Qabalist, however, has no such qualms.

How does the Jew regard the Gentile's adoption of his philosophy? Scholem, in his great work on Jewish mysticism, mentions Gentile occultists once only. 'From the brilliant misunderstandings of ... Eliphas Levi, to the highly coloured humbug of Aleister Crowley and his followers, the most eccentric and fantastic statements have been produced purporting to be legitimate interpretations of Qabalism.'[1] This is Scholem's only reference; it says a great deal. It is not our concern, however, to defend Judaism from Gentile heresy; suffice it to say that, in Gentile hands, the Qabalistic tradition has undergone extensive development.

The second major question to be asked is this: To what extent has the 'discovery' of Eastern monism during the past century or so influenced Western occultism? There is no doubt whatever that the influence has been profound and very extensive indeed; but let us not overstate the issue. Immanentism, and its accompanying pantheism, was a potent force at the beginning of the nineteenth century, and for some time later. It represented a reaction away from the unbridled transcendentalism of the deists on the one hand, and the Protestants on the other. Popular Protestantism has always tended towards an unbalanced transcendentalism and has usually frowned upon any immanentist manifestation within its ranks, Quakerism and quietism apart – and these are indeed apart from the main stream – Protestantism has produced practically nothing in the way of a mystical tradition whatever. The only Protestant mystic of any real renown is Jacob Boehme (1574-1624) who, although a Lutheran, exhibits not only Gnostic influences but also strongly Qabalistic as well! Boehme was almost certainly a Christian Qabalist, following in the footsteps of Paracelsus and Reuchlin.

Romantic pantheism gained massive support and a kind of authority from the exciting discoveries of Eastern scriptures by nineteenth-century scholars. Madame Blavatsky and her movement brought a strong monist influence home to the U.S.A. and this spread to Europe. Occultism flourished in the late nineteenth and early twentieth centuries, and we find such an exponent as W. B. Yeats, the poet, (long a member of 'the Hermetic Order of the Golden Dawn') embarking on a translation of the Upanishads, with the Indian scholar Shri Purohit Swami.

From our brief study of the theology of occultism in the first chapter of this section, however, we discover that, in Western hands, Hindu monism has broken its proper bounds. 'An immanent and transcendent God is the God of the magical philosophers,' we are told. Gareth Knight calls the Qabalah the 'Yoga of the West'. It is, he says, the backbone of the Western Mystery Tradition as opposed to that of the East. It is Western Hinduism, not Eastern.

From this point we are bound to ask what is meant by the 'Western Mystery Tradition'? This is a vague and ill-defined field of study. It is a matter of some bitterness among occultists that the mediaeval Church stamped out all pre-Christian speculation and practice with fire and sword. St Augustine was commanded by Pope Gregory to build his churches on the sites of pagan temples, thus transcending and redeeming the old religion. The mediaeval Church preferred the stake and the 'secular arm', to their profound discredit. Pre-Christian and non-Christian speculation was no doubt a grave threat to faith and morals, but miniature versions of the massacre of Montsegur were a poor way of setting forth the Gospel of Love.

Alchemy, rediscovered and restored to credibility by Jung, is perhaps the first ingredient in this tradition. The Rosicrucian myth is another; Knight pays some attention to both. Divination by astrology, by geomancy and by tarot was an important ingredient; divination by the contortion of burning sacrifice victims was another, ancient and less happy manifestation of the tradition. Witchcraft was common, both 'black' and 'white'.

It is important to realize that when the occultists speak of magic, it is white magic that they are talking about. The only occultist who does not deplore black magic is the black magician, and he is an aberration. However, we must realize that a control of the 'qliphothic' (demonic) is as much an attribute of the 'complete magician' as control of the healthy. A very important magical tradition is that of Abramelin the Mage who, after purification and perfection of his powers, invoked demonic forces as well as angelic. The magus must control *everything* after all! Crowley was a disciple of Abramelin; his purification and perfection are a matter for debate.

The magical tradition is, of course, most ancient, finding its roots in nature-worship in the hope that the corn would grow as a result. Pantheism is inherent in nature-worship, and Pantheism is inherent in all magical operations.

There were quasi-masonic traditions in plenty among the trade guilds, and freemasonry is a latter-day manifestation of this tradition, claiming Old Testament origins and standing very close to the occult traditions (although not all freemasons would hasten to describe themselves as occultists!) The Western Mystery Tradition is a multi-coloured hotch-potch, and folk-heroes like Arthur, Cuchulain and Robin Hood all have their place in it, along with the myths and heroes of Greek and Egyptian antiquity.

We may say, then, that the Qabalah, as we have found it in these pages, is a very eclectic affair indeed. Its philosophical framework is Jewish, and upon this framework has been hung all the rest, fitting together into a very remarkably coherent and all-embracing – or rather nearly-all-embracing – whole. It is a framework of symbolism, a pattern of archetypes; as such it is of considerable value, for it is of undoubted use to have at one's fingertips a coherent and generally credible guide to what must surely be THE STRUCTURE OF THE COLLECTIVE UNCONSCIOUS.

The collective unconscious is, of course, a term rather like electricity. We know what we mean by it, we do not know quite what it is. The term is capable of very much wider application than is often given to it. The whole evolutionary process from the hydrogen atom in inter-galactic space to man, is a process of the evolution, not merely of man as such, but of *consciousness*.

The term 'collective unconscious' can therefore validly extend a good deal further back than man as we now know him, and indeed this might be claimed to be verifiable by observation and experience. The collective unconscious, the *within* of the created order is the only realm in which pre-Christian religion and philosophy can possibly work. To say this is not to devalue them in the least, it is merely to keep them in their proper place. It is only the incarnation which transcends the collectivity of the created order; in it, manhood is taken up into God, as the Athanasian Creed makes clear. The incarnation is not merely the fulfilment of the Old Testament hope, it is that event, that reality, which makes sense of, and completes everything else.

Now, perhaps, we can see the relationship between the collective, the Brahman, the macrocosm, the world soul (and so forth), and the individual, the Atman, the microcosm, the individual soul. The relationship is very largely 'monistic', man is not a 'windowless monad', he partakes of the collective. There is no part of him that is not part of the gods – as long as the gods have a small 'g'. The collective unconscious is the realm of the gods and of the devils. (It may be the realm of the angels too, but it equally may not be.) The prince of this world ruled over it – this is the kingdom out of which he was cast by the incarnate life – the collective *within*. In Christ, all things are transformed and transfigured *from within*. Eastern and Western Hindus part company over the continuing reality of the individual, but within the limits set by the possibilities of a pre-incarnational worldview, their philosophy is profound.

Recognizing the Qabalah for what it is, a pattern of symbols and archetypes, a guide to the structure of both the macrocosmic collective unconscious and the microcosmic individual unconscious, the Christian can probably make considerable use of it. In the detachment which is possible to him because he is in the Christ and a partaker of his Life, he is able to accept the monism of the Qabalah because he is not committed to it *as theology*. It is merely an understanding of the relationship between the one and the whole *within* the created order. This understanding may be grief and tears to an occultist, but the purpose of this book is not the conversion of occultists to the faith so much as the presentation of an almost unknown, greatly misunderstood and very enlightening philosophy for the information of the already faithful.

There is much that could be argued and discussed at enormous length; there is much that seems incredible and bizarre and may, in fact be just that. But the main bones of the thing are now visible, the probable nature of the brute perceived, and we are now able to go ahead and see how it behaves when it is set in motion.

References

1   Scholem, p. 2

Appendix to Part Two

Symbols and attributes of the Sephiroth on the Tree of Life, taken from *The Mystical Qabalah* by Dion Fortune, with additional details from *A Practical Guide to Qabalistic Symbolism*, Volume One, by Gareth Knight.

Kether, The First Sephirah

Title: Kether, the Crown.

Magical Image: An ancient bearded king in profile.

Situation on the Tree: At the head of the Pillar of Equilibrium in the Supernal Triangle.

Titles given to Kether: Existence of Existences. Concealed of the Concealed. Ancient of Ancients. Ancient of Days. The Primordial Point. The Point within the Circle. The Most High. The Vast Countenance. The White Head. The Head which is not. *Macroprosopos.* Amen. *Lux Occulta. Lux Interna.* He.

God-Name: Eheih.

Archangel: Metatron.

Order of Angels: Holy Living Creatures.

Mundane Chakra: Primum Mobile. First Swirlings.

Spiritual Experience: Union with God.

Virtue: Attainment. Completion of the Great Work.

Vice: None.

Correspondence in Microcosm: The cranium. The sah. Yechidah. The divine spark. The thousand-petalled lotus.

Symbols: The point. The point within a circle. The crown. The swastika.

Tarot Cards: The four aces:

> Ace of wands – root of the powers of fire.
> Ace of cups – root of the powers of water.
> Ace of swords – root of the powers of air.
> Ace of pentacles – root of the powers of earth.

The Flashing Colours:

> Colour in Atziluth: Brilliance.
> Colour in Briah: Pure white brilliance.
> Colour in Yetzirah: Pure white brilliance.
> Colour in Assiah: White, flecked gold.

Chokmah, The Second Sephirah

Title: Chokmah, Wisdom.

Magical Image: A bearded male figure.

Situation on the Tree: At the head of the Pillar of Mercy in the Supernal Triangle.

Titles given to Chokmah: Power of Yetzirah. Ab. Abba. The Supernal Father. Tetragrammaton. Yod of Tetragrammaton.

God-Name: Jehovah or Jah (as 'Jehovah' is, in the Old Testament, a devotional device, combining the consonants of Yahweh with the vowels of Elohim, no doubt those Qabalists who are aware of this mean 'Yahweh').

Archangel: Ratziel.

Order of Angels: Auphanim. Wheels.

Mundane Chakra: Mazloth, the Zodiac.

Spiritual Experience: The Vision of God face to face.

Virtue: Devotion.

Vice: None.

Correspondence in Microcosm: The left side of the face.

Symbols: The lingam. The phallus. The yod of tetragrammaton. The inner robe of glory. The standing-stone. The tower. The uplifted rod of power. The straight line.

Tarot Cards: The four twos:

Two of wands – dominion.

Two of cups – love.

Two of swords – peace restored.

Two of pentacles – harmonious change.

The Flashing Colours:

Colour in Atziluth: Pure soft blue.

Colour in Briah: Grey.

Colour in Yetzirah: Pearl-grey, iridescent.

Colour in Assiah: White flecked with red, blue and yellow.

Binah, The Third Sephirah

ב

Title: Binah, Understanding.

Magical Image: A mature woman. A matron.

Situation on the Tree: At the head of the Pillar of Severity in the Supernal Triangle.

Titles given to Binah: Ama, the dark sterile Mother. Aima, the bright fertile Mother. Khorsia, the Throne. Marah, the Great Sea.

God-Name: Jehovah Elohim.

Archangel: Tzaphkiel.

Order of Angels: Aralim, Thrones.

Mundane Chakra: Shabbathai, Saturn.

Spiritual Experience: Vision of Sorrow.

Virtue: Silence.

Vice: Avarice.

Correspondence in Microcosm: The right side of the face.

Symbols: The yoni. The kteis. The vesica piscis. The cup or chalice. The outer robe of concealment.

Tarot Cards: The four threes:

Three of wands – established strength.

Three of cups – abundance.

Three of swords – sorrow.

Three of pentacles – material works.

The Flashing Colours:

Colour in Atziluth: Crimson.

Colour in Briah: Black.

Colour in Yetzirah: Dark brown.

Colour in Assiah: Grey flecked with pink.

Daath, The Hidden Sephirah

●

Title: Daath, Knowledge.

Magical Image: A head with two faces, looking both ways.

Situation on the Tree: At a point where the Abyss bisects the Middle Pillar.

Titles given to Daath: The Invisible Sephirah. The Hidden or Unrevealed Cosmic Mind. The Mystical Sephirah. The Upper Room.

God-Name: A conjunction of Jehovah (Yahweh) and Elohim.

Archangel: The Archangels of the Cardinal Points.

Order of Angels: Serpents.

Mundane Chakra: Sothis or Sirius, the Dog Star.

Spiritual Experience: Vision across the Abyss.

Virtue: Detachment. Perfection of Justice and the application of the Virtues untainted by Personality considerations. Confidence in the future.

Vice: Doubt of the future. Apathy. Inertia. Cowardice (fear of the future). Pride (leading to isolation and disintegration).

Correspondence in Microcosm: The throat.

Symbols: The condemned cell. The prism. The empty room. The sacred mountain. A grain of corn. The complete absence of symbol.

Tarot Cards: None.

The Flashing Colours:

Colour in Atziluth: Lavender.

Colour in Briah: Silvery grey.

Colour in Yetzirah: Pure violet.

Colour in Assiah: Grey, flecked with yellow.

Chesed, The Fourth Sephirah

♃

Title: Chesed, Mercy.
Magical Image: A mighty crowned and throned King.
Situation on the Tree: In the centre of the Pillar of Mercy.
Titles given to Chesed: Gedulah. Love. Majesty.
God-Name: El.
Archangel: Tzadkiel.
Order of Angels: Chasmalim. Brilliant Ones.
Mundane Chakra: Tzedek. Jupiter.
Spiritual Experience: Vision of Love.
Virtue: Obedience.
Vice: Bigotry. Hypocrisy. Gluttony. Tyranny.
Correspondence in Microcosm: The left arm. .
Symbols: The solid figure. Tetrahedron. Pyramid. Equal-armed cross. Orb.
  Wand. Sceptre. Crook.
Tarot Cards: The four fours:
  Four of wands – Perfected work.
  Four of cups – Pleasure.
  Four of swords – Rest from strife.
  Four of pentacles – Earthly power.
The Flashing Colours:
  Colour in Atziluth: Deep violet.
  Colour in Briah: Blue.
  Colour in Yetzirah: Deep purple.
  Colour in Assiah: Deep azure, flecked yellow.

Geburah, The Fifth Sephirah

♂

Title: Geburah. Strength. Severity.
Magical Image: A mighty warrior in his chariot.
Situation on the Tree: In the centre of the Pillar of Severity.
Titles given to Geburah: Din – Justice. Pachad – fear.
God-Name: Elohim Gebor.
Archangel: Khamael.
Order of Angels: Seraphim. Fiery Serpents.
Mundane Chakra: Madim. Mars.
Spiritual Experience: Vision of Power.
Virtue: Energy. Courage.
Vice: Cruelty. Destruction.
Correspondence in Microcosm: The right arm.
Symbols: The pentagon. The five-petalled Tudor rose. The sword. The spear. The scourge. The chain.
Tarot Cards: The four fives:
 Five of wands – Strife.
 Five of cups – Loss in pleasure.
 Five of swords – Defeat.
 Five of pentacles – Earthly trouble.
The Flashing Colours:
 Colour in Atziluth: Orange.
 Colour in Briah: Scarlet red.
 Colour in Yetzirah: Bright scarlet.
 Colour in Assiah: Red, flecked with black.

Tiphareth, The Sixth Sephirah

⊙

Title: Tiphareth. Beauty.

Magical Image: A majestic king. A child. A sacrificed god.

Situation on the Tree: In the centre of the Pillar of Equilibrium (or Consciousness).

Titles given to Tiphareth: Zoar Anpin – the Lesser Countenance. Melekh – the King. Adam. The Son. The Man.

God-Name: Tetragrammaton Aloah Va Daath.

Archangel: Raphael.

Order of Angels: Malachim, Kings.

Mundane Chakra: Shemesh, the Sun.

Spiritual Experience: Vision of the harmony of things. Mysteries of the Crucifixion.

Virtue: Devotion to the Great Work.

Vice: Pride.

Correspondence in Microcosm: The breast.

Symbols: The lamen. The rosy cross. The Calvary cross. The truncated pyramid. The cube.

Tarot Cards: The four sixes:

Six of wands – Victory.

Six of cups – Joy.

Six of swords – Earned success.

Six of Pentacles – Material success.

The Flashing Colours:

Colour in Atziluth: Clear rose-pink.

Colour in Briah: Yellow.

Colour in Yetzirah: Rich salmon-pink.

Colour in Assiah: Golden amber.

Netzach, The Seventh Sephirah

♀

Title: Netzach. Victory.
Magical Image: A beautiful naked woman.
Situation on the Tree: At the foot of the Pillar of Mercy.
Titles given to Netzach: Firmness. Valour.
God-Name: Jehovah Tzabaoth; the Lord of Hosts.
Archangel: Haniel.
Order of Angels: Elohim, gods.
Mundane Chakra: Nogah, Venus.
Spiritual Experience: Vision of beauty triumphant.
Virtue: Unselfishness.
Vice: Unchastity. Lust.
Correspondence in Microcosm: Loins, hips and legs.
Symbols: Lamp and girdle. The rose.
Tarot Cards: the four sevens:
    Seven of wands – Valour.
    Seven of cups – Illusory success.
    Seven of swords – Unstable effort.
    Seven of pentacles – Success unfulfilled.
The Flashing Colours:
    Colour in Atziluth: Amber.
    Colour in Briah: Emerald.
    Colour in Yetzirah: Bright yellowish green.
    Colour in Assiah: Olive, flecked with gold.

Hod, The Eighth Sephirah

Title: Hod, Glory.
Magical Image: An hermaphrodite.
Situation on the Tree: At the foot of the Pillar of Severity.
Titles given to Hod: None.
God-Name: Elohim Tzabaoth, the God of Hosts.
Archangel: Michael.
Order of Angels: Beni Elohim, Sons of God.
Mundane Chakra: Kokab, Mercury.
Spiritual Experience: Vision of Splendour.
Virtue: Truthfulness.
Vice: Falsehood. Dishonesty.
Correspondence in Microcosm: Loins and legs.
Symbols: Names. Versicles. Apron.
Tarot Cards: The four eights:
    Eight of wands – Swiftness.
    Eight of cups – Abandoned success.
    Eight of swords – Shortened force.
    Eight of pentacles – Prudence.
The Flashing Colours:
    Colour in Atziluth: Violet-purple.
    Colour in Briah: Orange.
    Colour in Yetzirah: Russet-red.
    Colour in Assiah: Yellowish black, flecked with white.

Yesod, The Ninth Sephirah

☾

Title: Yesod, the Foundation.

Magical Image: A beautiful naked man, very strong.

Situation on the Tree: Towards the base of the Pillar of Equilibrium of Consciousness.

Titles given to Yesod: The Treasure-house of Images.

God-Name: Shaddai el Chai, the Almighty Living God.

Archangel: Gabriel.

Order of Angels: Kerubim, the Strong.

Mundane Chakra: Levanah, the Moon.

Spiritual Experience: Vision of the Machinery of the Universe.

Virtue: Independence.

Vice: Idleness.

Correspondence in Microcosm: Reproductive organs.

Symbols: The perfumes and sandals.

Tarot Cards: The four nines:

　　Nine of wands – Great strength.

　　Nine of cups – Material happiness.

　　Nine of swords – Despair and cruelty.

　　Nine of pentacles – Material gain.

The Flashing Colours:

　　Colour in Atziluth: Indigo.

　　Colour in Briah: Violet.

　　Colour in Yetzirah: Very dark purple.

　　Colour in Assiah: Citrine, flecked with azure.

Malkuth, The Tenth Sephirah

Title: Malkuth, the Kingdom.

Magical Image: A young woman, crowned and throned.

Situation on the Tree: At the base of the Pillar of Equilibrium or Consciousness.

Titles given to Malkuth: The Gate. The Gate of Death. The Gate of the Shadow of Death. The Gate of Tears. The Gate of Justice. The Gate of Prayer. The Gate of the Daughter of the Mighty Ones. The Gate of the Garden of Eden. The Inferior Mother. Malkah, the Queen. Kallah, the Bride. The Virgin.

God-Name: Adonai Malekh, or Adonai ha Aretz.

Archangel: Sandalphon.

Order of Angels: Ashim, Souls of Fire.

Mundane Chakra: Cholem ha Yesodoth, Sphere of the Elements.

Spiritual Experience: Vision of the Holy Guardian Angel. (Knight gives: 'Knowledge and Conversation of the Holy Guardian Angel'.)

Virtue: Discrimination.

Vice: Avarice. Inertia.

Correspondence in Microcosm: The feet. The anus.

Symbols: Altar of the double cube. The equal-armed cross. The magic circle. The triangle of art, or of evocation.

Tarot Cards: The four tens:

    Ten of wands – Oppression.

    Ten of cups – Perfected success.

    Ten of swords – Ruin.

    Ten of pentacles – Wealth.

The Flashing Colours:

    Colour in Atziluth: Yellow.

    Colour in Briah: Citrine, olive, russet and black.

    Colour in Yetzirah: Citrine, olive, russet, and black flecked with gold.

    Colour in Assiah: Black, rayed with yellow.

PART THREE

THE SEARCH FOR SELF-REALIZATION

The Idea of Self-Realization

IN the year 1965, the Italian psychiatrist Roberto Assagioli published an exposition of the main principles and techniques of the school of professional thought and practice which he represents, and in which he is a leading figure. The title of his book is *Psychosynthesis*, and this title correctly suggests the approach to the whole subject of psychotherapy which the Doctor advocates. In brief, he is not concerned with a mere 'running repair' approach, he seeks a synthesis, a completion of the whole man, a self-realization on the part of his patient.

Almost at once, his book which, in spite of its title, is lucid and readable as well as being learned and exhaustively documented, was hailed in a number of occult circles as a breakthrough. Here was a practising psychiatrist who spoke their language and whose clinical, empirical approach seemed to bear out and massively support the conclusions – and even more, the techniques – of their speculative philosophy.

Doctor Assagioli, like the Qabalists, has a liking for helpful diagrams which illustrate his thesis. (The Tree of Life is the Qabalists' 'helpful diagram'.) It will be very much worth our while to quote the Doctor at some length; the terms which he uses, and the meaning of those terms, will be of fundamental interest to us as we proceed with our investigation of occult practice (as opposed to the theory). After an exhaustive citation of authorities Assagioli writes:

'This vast amount of studies and research offers enough material for an attempt at co-ordination and synthesis. If we assemble ascertained facts, positive and well-authenticated contributions and well-founded interpretations, ignoring the exaggerations and theoretical superstructures of the various schools, we arrive at a pluridimensional conception of the human personality which, though far from perfect or final is, we think, more inclusive and nearer to reality than previous formulations. To illustrate such a conception of the constitution of the human being in his living concrete reality the following diagram may be helpful. It is, of course, a crude and elementary picture that can give only a structural, static, almost 'anatomical' representation of our inner constitution, while it leaves out its dynamic aspect, which is the most important and essential one. But here, as in every science, gradual steps must be taken and progressive approximations be made. When dealing with a reality so plastic and elusive as our psychological life, it is important not to lose sight of the main lines and of the fundamental differences; otherwise the multiplicity of details is liable to obscure the picture as a whole and to prevent our realizing the respective significance, purpose, and value of its different parts. With these reservations and qualifications, the chart is as follows:' [1]

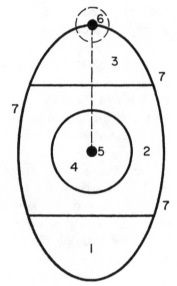

1. The Lower Unconscious
2. The Middle Unconscious
3. The Higher Unconscious or Superconscious
4. The Field of Consciousness
5. The Conscious Self or 'I'
6. The Higher Self
7. The Collective Unconscious

It will be helpful to spend a little time elaborating on the meaning of the terms which are numbered One to Seven above. Doctor Assagioli describes them as follows:

1. *The Lower Unconscious.* This contains:
   (a) The elementary psychological activities which direct the life of the body; the intelligent co-ordination of bodily functions.
   (b) The fundamental drives and primitive urges.
   (c) Many complexes, charged with intense emotion.
   (d) Dreams and imaginations of an inferior kind.
   (e) Lower, uncontrolled parapsychological processes.
   (f) Various pathological manifestations, such as phobias, obsessions, compulsive urges and paranoid delusions.

2. *The Middle Unconscious.* This is formed of psychological elements similar to those of our waking consciousness and easily accessible to it.

In this inner region our various experiences are assimilated, our ordinary mental and imaginative activities are elaborated and developed in a sort of psychological gestation before their birth into the light of consciousness.

3. *The Higher Unconscious or Superconscious.* From this region we receive our higher intuitions and inspirations – artistic, philosophical or scientific, ethical 'imperatives' and urges to humanitarian and heroic action. It is the source of the higher feelings, such as altruistic love; of genius and of the states of contemplation, illumination and ecstasy. In this realm are latent the higher psychic functions and spiritual energies.

4. *The Field of Consciousness.* This term – which is not quite accurate but which is clear and convenient for practical purposes – is used to designate that part of our personality of which we are directly aware: the incessant flow of sensations, images, thoughts, feelings, desires, and impulses which we can observe, analyse and judge.

5. *The Conscious Self or 'I'.* The 'self', that is to say, the point of pure self-awareness, is often confused with the conscious personality just described, but in reality it is quite different from it. This can be ascertained by the use of careful introspection. The changing *contents* of our consciousness (the sensations, thoughts, feelings, etc.) are one thing, while the 'I', the self, the *centre* of our consciousness is another ... But the 'man in the street' and even many well-educated people do not take the trouble to observe themselves and to discriminate; they drift on the surface of the 'mind-stream' and identify themselves with its successive waves, with the changing contents of their consciousness.

6. *The Higher Self.* (This, Assagioli emphasizes in a footnote, should not be confused in any way with the super-ego of Freud.) The conscious self is generally not only submerged in the ceaseless flow of psychological contents but seems to disappear altogether when we fall asleep, when we faint, when we are under the effect of an anaesthetic or narcotic, or in a state of hypnosis. And when we awake the self mysteriously re-appears, we do not know how or whence – a fact which, if closely examined, is truly baffling and disturbing. This leads us to assume that the reappearance of the conscious self or ego is due to the existence of a permanent centre, of a true self situated beyond or 'above' it. There are various ways by means of which the reality of the self can be ascertained. There have been many individuals who have achieved, more or less temporarily, a conscious realization of the self that for them has the same degree of certainty as is experienced by an explorer who has entered a previously unknown region ... Then we have the corroboration of such philosophers as Kant and

Herbart who make a clear distinction between the empirical ego and the noumenal or real self. This self is above, and unaffected by, the flow of the mind-stream or by bodily considerations; and the personal conscious self should be considered merely as its reflection, its 'projection' in the field of the personality. At the present stage of psychological investigation little is definitely known concerning the self, but the importance of this synthesizing centre well warrants further research.

7. *The Collective Unconscious.* Human beings are not isolated, they are not 'monads without windows' as Leibnitz thought. They may at times feel subjectively isolated, but the extreme existentialistic conception is not true, either psychologically or spiritually. The outer line of the oval of the diagram should be regarded as 'delimiting' but not as 'dividing'. It should be regarded as analogous to the membrane delimiting a cell, which permits a constant and active interchange with the whole body to which the cell belongs. Processes of 'psychological osmosis' are going on all the time, both with other human beings and with the general psychic environment. The latter corresponds to what Jung has called the 'collective unconscious'; but he has not clearly defined this term, in which he includes elements of different, even opposite natures, namely primitive archaic structures and higher, forward-directed activities of a superconscious character. [2]

We have quoted the doctor at some length, and we shall find ourselves returning to his book at intervals throughout the remainder of this section of our study. Already the relevance of his empirical and clinical approach is apparent; already there are correspondences of thought, although with different terminology. Already there is much in what we have quoted to arrest the attention of both Christian and Qabalist.

The doctor claims that his diagram, thus explained, helps us to reconcile what seem to be contradicting facts and experiences; first, the apparent duality, the seeming existence of two selves in us, and at the same time the real unity and uniqueness of the self. He is concerned with putting the understanding at which he has arrived to work in the practical business of psychotherapy. 'In our ordinary life: he continues, 'we are limited and bound in a thousand ways – the prey of illusions and phantasms, the slaves of unrecognized complexes, tossed hither and thither by external influences, blinded and hypnotized by deceiving appearances. No wonder then that man, in such a state, is often discontented, insecure and changeable in his moods, thoughts and actions. Feeling intuitively that he is "one", and yet finding that he is "divided unto himself", he is bewildered and fails to understand either himself or others. No wonder that he, not knowing or understanding himself, has no self-control and is continually involved in his own mistakes and weaknesses; that so many lives are failures, or are at least limited and saddened by diseases of mind or body, or tormented by doubt, discouragement and despair.'[3]

He proceeds to ask whether and how the central problem of human life may be solved. Self-realization is the goal he sets for himself and his patients, and the techniques and approaches to his profession which occupy the remaining three hundred or so pages of his book, he describes as 'Psychosynthesis: the formation or reconstruction of the personality around the new centre' (The true self).[4]

Self-realization is the heading of this section of our book. It is the quest of man throughout the ages, and ever on a deeper level. The flood of literature on Yoga in its many and varied forms, and the growing interest in all matters concerning the occult, to which Jung bore witness as we saw in the first introductory essay, are all manifestations of the deep desire of bewildered modern man to find himself and discover what he is for and what he is about. The fundamental desire is a profoundly healthy one; the means employed are sometimes less healthy.

The revelations of the unconscious mind are an obsession with modern man; probing the depths of the unconscious has become one of the great quests of the age, although not all those on the quest realize that that is what they are doing. Here is a great cavern open at our feet, what does it contain? More important still, *where does it lead?* This is the great speculation-point for Qabalist and Hindu alike, and for more than these alone. Where does it lead? To God? What answers shall we find to the great questions of life? Will our new science explain away 'religion'? What place has the idea of transcendence in this new field of research and exploration?

The great difficulty that present-day man experiences with the very idea of transcendence, and his increasing preoccupation with the idea of immanence (and the pantheism which is never far away) is a symptom of the same basic questioning. To many observers, this whole trend is of the devil; it is the belief behind this present work that it is rather of the Holy Spirit. Doubts and questionings must always precede a newer, deeper understanding; the believer who has never doubted has never really believed; the 'dark nights' have a wider application than mere individual spirituality. Man, even at prayer, is in no sense whatever a 'monad without windows'. The stirrings of the one and of the many are very deeply connected. Not for nothing, for example, does the New Testament speak of the Church as 'salt' and 'leaven'.

In the growing and developing individual, self-realization manifests itself in a number of formal, conventional and quite superficial ways. Ability to grow a beard indicates that puberty is past; it does not, however, indicate patriarchal wisdom. The growing man, in the initial uncertainty of his manhood, will be obsessed with a desire to 'look the part'. The part must be both looked and acted, and the one helps the other. The newly commissioned subaltern will grow a suitably military moustache; the young commuter who is 'something in the city' will acquire a bowler hat, an umbrella, and a suit that exactly conforms to unspoken conventions about the kind of suits worn by young men who are 'something in the city'. There will be, at times, an almost hysterical avoidance of the unconventional, and thus unacceptable. This will, however, be a largely subjective reaction because the genuinely unconventional will often provoke secret admiration in that they are 'characters' in their own right.

The insecure young man must 'conform to an image'. The image must be one that is acceptable, a stereotype. This is no new thing, it has been ever thus; modern methods of communications have only underlined this already well-established phenomenon. Teenagers, in revolt against the older generation (a venerable phenomenon if ever there was one) will go to some lengths to do violence to the image against which they are currently in revolt. In the process they will invariably conform to other, counter-images, with a slavishness that at least rivals the slavishness against which they are rebelling. Life, on its superficial, television-commercial level – the level at which millions of the 'men in the street' of which Assagioli speaks are content to live it – is reduced to a series of exercises in conformity to fashionable stereotypes. The stereotypes are represented by pop-idols, disc-jockeys, male and female models, sporting personalities, actors and actresses and so on. This is a kind of self-realization, a necessary kind, but on the lowest possible level. This is the level on which conformity bestows confidence. Look the part and you may be able to feel the part. Others may accept you *as* the part. Keep up with the Joneses and people may think you *are* the Joneses. This is the self-realization of the suburbs.

Self-realization begins to be really sought after from the moment when mere social image-conformity begins to pall; when its utter irrelevance to life proper begins to be perceived. It is interesting, and it is probably significant, that the awakening interest in the unconscious, in Yoga, in the occult, in self-realization in general, is most manifest in those suburbs of Europe and America in which a former Protestant and transcendentalist Christianity has given place to a general indifference and agnosticism on the part of the great mass of society. The decay of an incomplete and unbalanced expression of the Christian revelation has left more than just a vacuum; an individualistic and often sentimental piety has, in its collapse, opened the door to a reality-denying monism by way of reaction. The quasi-religious drug movement – manifesting itself in just this type of society – has given impetus and a semblance of authority to monistic philosophies, and the theology of the successors of transcendentalist Protestantism has displayed a growing preoccupation with the immanent to the almost total exclusion of the transcendent. Self-realization, by Yoga, by the occult, by psycho-analysis and by LSD is the order of the day.

Self-realization, under all those headings, involves us in meditation. Meditation itself is becoming a matter of increasing interest at the present time – but not within the Church. Within the Catholic tradition of Christianity there is at the present time a widespread move away from meditation as strictly understood and towards a simpler prayer of quiet or contemplation. We shall return to this matter in due course, but we are not at the moment concerned so much with what is happening within the Church as with what is happening outside it.

It will be our main intention, in the chapters which follow, to examine the various techniques of meditation which are common to Yoga, to occultism and – as we shall see – to psycho-analysis. We shall see the points of divergence from the Christian's mental prayer, and we shall discover that the meditational techniques we have mentioned all tend towards 'changes in consciousness' and are thus, by definition, magical in character.

Without tying ourselves down to any kind of closed system of thought, nor identifying too closely Doctor Assagioli's little diagram with the Qabalist's Tree of Life, we may perhaps identify Self-realization and the attainment of the true or higher self, as the doctor understands it, with the attainment of 'Tiphareth consciousness' and the knowledge and conversation of the Holy Guardian Angel in the Qabalistic scheme of things. The point is capable of vigorous debate, but we shall keep it in mind as a kind of working hypothesis in the pages that follow.

Also to be kept in our minds as we proceed with our investigation of occult meditation and practice is the question; 'What is the end in view?' This may be more vulgarly expressed as 'So what?' This is a question that must not be lost sight of. Before we have done, we must try to answer it.

References

1   Roberto Assagioli, *Psychosynthesis*, Hobbs, Dorman & Co Inc. N.Y, p. 16
2   Roberto Assagioli, *Psychosynthesis*, pp. 17-19
3   Roberto Assagioli, *Psychosynthesis*, p. 20
4   Roberto Assagioli, *Psychosynthesis*, p. 21

Me, My and Mine

'STAND facing east. Raise the right hand and say, out loud or mentally, "In Thy hands is the kingdom, the power and the glory" – as you do so making the sign of the cross with the right hand – "for ever and ever, amen," clasping the hands together. Keeping the right arm straight, first and second fingers extended in line with it, lift it somewhat above the horizontal, and draw in the air before you the sign of the pentagram or five pointed star. The last movement will bring it down so that the fingers are pointing at the centre of the star and say, "In the name of (God Name of Sephirah) I open the east." Now move round to the south, keeping the arm extended so that the fingers describe a quarter circle and there repeat the pentagram, but this time say, "In the name of — I open the south." In the same way, move round to the west and north, repeating the pentagram at each of these points. Complete the circle by returning to the east. The circle and pentagrams should be visualized as blazing in the air with a golden light. Open the arms wide, parallel to the floor, and say, "In the east, Raphael ; in the west, Gabriel; In the south, Michael; In the north, Uriel. About me flame the pentagrams, behind me shines the six-rayed star. (Drop the left hand and raise the right to make the sign of the cross as before), and above my head is the Glory of God, in whose hands is the kingdom, the power and the glory, for ever and ever, amen."' [1]

The 'opening ritual' thus described (there is a 'closing ritual' too) is very far removed from gibberish. The whole exercise is one of focusing the faculties, and the symbols and gestures are directed to that end. Everything is visualized strongly and in colour. It is an exercise in the direction of concentration, and the symbols are the most potent known to the Qabalist for getting the thing off, morally, on what he considers to be the right foot. It is, however, immediately apparent who is the centre of this colourful exercise. It is 'ME'.

The occultist's theology is a hotch-potch. It relies heavily on the traditions of Hinduism which are themselves highly speculative and full of contradictions. The whole ethos, theologically speaking, is one of widely differing 'do it yourself'. Theology, however is not the main concern of the occultist; results are what he seeks, not the reasoning behind them. Above all else, occultism stands or falls by the *experience* it provides. In everything experience is the criterion; in ceremonial magic, in solitary meditation, it is always experience that is sought. The occultist is one who, deliberately and seriously 'lives for kicks' because the 'kicks' are, to him, all part and parcel of the Great Work of enlarging his consciousness to the power infinity.

Thus stated, the pitfalls are glaring. The most degenerate kind of spiritual sensuality threatens, but the more responsible teachers of occultism are insistent in their warnings. This is a serious business – an exact and scientific business, it is claimed. Occultism is hard and dedicated work and lodge discipline can be very strict. Occultism is multi-coloured and manifests itself in many forms (only one of which is our present concern), and it is a happy hunting ground for the eccentric. It should not be imagined, however, that it is a field inhabited only by the eccentric, the erotic and the dangerous. The public image of occultism as an amalgam of lunacy and 'black magic' is very wide of the mark.

The desire for direct experience, and the claim to be able to provide it, is not confined to occult lodges. It is the loud and insistent cry of the newly founded 'psychedelic churches' in the U.S.A. that their use of such drugs as mescaline and LSD represents a breakthrough, via body chemistry, to direct mystical experience. The use of drugs such as these is not 'escapist' but 'exploratory' and essentially religious, they claim. The Neo-American Church is dedicated to 'the appreciation of transcendental reality'. The more middle-class Church of the Awakening recognizes that 'even psychedelic religion has both an internal and an external function – the latter to be expressed in terms of "love", "service" and "growth"'.[2] It is the claim of the LSD-user that his practice gives *results*. The orthodox churches, he claims, must look to their laurels; they are not delivering the goods in terms of *direct experience*. Modern man is disillusioned, even with his own empiricism, even with the science which he worships. It does not deliver ultimate goods. Modern man wants *the direct experience of reality*.

The LSD-user and the occultist are talking the same language and seeking the same thing. They seek the experience of reality. There is a moral distinction – an utterly vital moral distinction between the search for the experience of reality and the search for the reality as it is in itself! This distinction, extraordinarily hard to grasp, and in practice, almost impossible to maintain, unaided by grace, is the 'great divide' between mysticism and magic.

The LSD-user and the occultist speak of mystical experience and mysticism. *In fact it is magical experience and magic!* The distinction is very difficult to appreciate; magical experience is very profound, there is nothing intrinsically evil about it, it is a built-in possibility for all men. It is, in fact, the subjective counterpart to much objective, transcendent experience. A 'mystical experience' – a thing notoriously difficult of definition – is wholly objective in character and 'says' something to the person receiving it. It is necessary for the human faculties to find expression, in sensory terms, for the transcendent communication.

This is the subjective counterpart of the objective reality. There is, in fact, a perceptible 'time-lag' between the contact with reality in itself and the subjective expression. The two complement each other, but there is no mistaking the distinction. The man who has had such an experience (and many have) will know exactly what is meant here. The man who has not had such an experience will not know what is being talked about! Alas! but there it is!

The subjective experience is psychological, or, to use another term, essentially *magical* in character. It represents an enlargement of the finite consciousness; the enlargement of which – at will – is the whole essence and meaning of magic. The LSD-user has 'slipped the cables' and returned to an almost innocent awareness of the unity of things. His is an intensely pantheistic experience because it is intensely subjective. All the 'stuff' with which the sensory faculties respond to the transcendent is alerted and unrestrained. He has returned in the direction of 'OM' – which is the opposite direction to 'OMEGA'. It represents the difference between 'childish' and 'child-like', and that difference is very profound indeed.

The occultist, although he seeks experience as does the LSD-user, is in a somewhat different category. He seeks his experience the hard way and, he believes, the legitimate and truly effective way. In the meditative magic which will be our main concern, he seeks his results by a very disciplined concentration on basic symbols; shapes, concepts and colours. These, he rightly considers, are the modes of expression of the unconscious mind. Using the Qabalah and its related symbolism as his 'plan of attack', he seeks to tread the paths from Sephirah to Sephirah, thus attaining a comprehensive and all-embracing consciousness. This approach is shrewd, simple and without much doubt exceedingly rewarding to the determined occultist – *within its limitations*. Speaking, as he does, of 'a tree in every Sephirah', he is, in a sense, only dealing with the 'tree in Malkuth'. Even Crowley did not imagine that he would attain the fullness of deity in one incarnation! The limits, however, are not easily perceived by the occultist, indeed it is very probable that his perception is inhibited. He is seeking to plunge into the unconscious – and indeed *into the collective unconscious*.

Assagioli's diagram, and its explanation, reveals to us that there is no impenetrable barrier between the individual unconscious and the collective; indeed he speaks of an 'osmosis', a coming and going, with a membrane-like delimitation between the individual and the collective. If we use the Hindu terms Atman and Brahman for the individual 'higher self' and its related conscious and unconscious mind, and the 'collective self', the sum of all the 'within' of creation, we can see both the profundity and the truth – and the limitations – of Hinduism. If for Atman and Brahman we substitute microcosm and Macrocosm we can see the same of occultism. We see, too, just why there is a kind of 'closed circuit', constricting atmosphere about them both. The universe, endless though it is, is nevertheless *finite*. Creation is not God; creation can only be rightly understood as being IN God.

We must return to the all-important distinction between seeking the experience of reality, and seeking reality as it is in itself. The Christian who is educated in mystical theology, and possessed of some experience of its workings, will recognize this distinction as fundamental. Indeed, the dark nights, the deserts, the aridities, the sufferings generally of those called to be Christians, be they 'mystics' or not, have as their quite clear and specific intention, the ridding of the human will of the very last shreds of attachment to 'experience' as such, and the refinement and purification of that will until it seeks God as he is in himself, and not the 'experience' of him.

It is the mystic who suffers perhaps more than most because the 'experience' side of mystical prayer is so utterly sublime. There is no 'experience' more transcendently blessed than, for example, that way of mystical prayer called ecstatic union. There is no desolation more black than when, having been favoured with this prayer, it is utterly withdrawn! And the reason it is utterly withdrawn is that the mystic must have his will purified all over again to seek – not 'ecstatic union', but GOD! The pain of this discipline is terrible.

It will be seen now, that the meditation of the occultist and the prayer of the Christian, although they seem to have many points in common – and Gareth Knight quotes St John of the Cross most plausibly – *are in fact two utterly separate undertakings*. It would be misleading to say that they aim in opposite directions. It would be wrong to claim, *a priori*, that no occultist could possibly find God. God is not limited. Occultists vary in their inner motives like everyone else. Some (Crowley?) are determined to *be* God. Some (Fortune?) are determined to *find* God. We must avoid judgement; but it is morally necessary for an occultist, sensing a dead-end and seeking escape and fulfilment in Christ, to 'become as a little child';

to lay aside all his past experience, however meaningful and profound, and *start all over again*. On a rimless wheel, one cannot jump from spoke to spoke; one has to go back to the hub.

There is a good deal of magic on the mystical path; it is incidental and must be transcended. There is a good deal of ceremonial magic in the Church's Liturgy, and it has its rightful place therein. It must, however, be transcended. The ecclesiastical ceremonarius (of which there are not a few) must beware that he does not become a mere ceremonial magician! The enthusiast who hurls himself into the latest liturgical experiment as a matter of course, or who waxes eloquent about 'the jolly good High Mass that they do at St Frideswides!' is not far removed from Dion Fortune who spoke so spine-chillingly of 'working the Mass with power' because of the employment of the proper 'magical principles'. The austere Protestant who accuses his Catholic brother of 'magic' is often right, but he is usually wrong in employing that word as polemic. Magic is more modernly described as psychology and as such it is respectable. It is in fact essential since man must express himself in meaningful movement and gesture. The Liturgy has about it both drama and dance; but the mere connoisseur of ceremonial (a rarer bird than he was), who seeks *experience* in the Liturgy, and whose devotion never quite transcends the performance to perceive the reality, will remain at a low, magical level of awareness and sooner or later fall even from that. His search for experience will extend even to his Communion; it is a high quest for a cosy glow, and is doomed to unfulfilment.

The next few chapters will concern themselves with techniques and specific practices. There is a great deal that will be meaningful and relevant to the Christian's prayers. There is a great deal that is valuable in its own right *when rightly perceived for what it is*. Magic, over the centuries, has blossomed into science. There is much in occultism that is at this moment on the borderline.

References

1   Gareth Knight, Vol. I, pp. 240-1
2   William Braden, *The Private Sea*, p. 214

Prayer or Probe?

A CRITICISM of the Western Church that may be made in all fairness is that it has seriously neglected to teach the great mass of the faithful about the many and varied ways in which prayer may be done. There are tens of thousands of Christians who have received no instruction at all on this subject. There is a great deal of exhortation, but actual instruction – almost never. Pulpit guidance is normally of the kind which generally exhorts the faithful to see to it that a right proportion of adoration, thanksgiving, penance, intercession and petition enter into their prayer life. The crying need is not for a detached and academic lecture in cake making so much as a rolling up of the sleeves and practical, individual guidance.

The practical difficulties are great, but there are indications that, in this matter at any rate, the tide is turning; however it is an unhappy fact that large numbers of Christians will still be simply 'left to get on with it', and allowed to assume that the sum total of prayer is 'me talking to God', an operation which can only be performed when the body is in a kneeling position!

Large numbers of Christian souls will still be nagged by the sheer unreality that this can engender, ignorant of the fact that the *ways of praying* are legion and that it is in no way meritorious to struggle to maintain recollection in acute discomfort merely for appearances sake. The one good thing that this ignorant and neglectful approach to the teaching of prayer can claim to its credit is that it has at least shown that *the basic reality of prayer is an act of will*, seeking to conform the human will to that of God.

The occultist and his Eastern brother, the follower of Yoga, have much, not so much to teach us, as to remind us. They are sensitive to what we might describe as the *psychosomatic* aspects of prayer. They teach common sense and its application as a discipline. They remember what so many self-styled teachers of prayer forget, that elementary, basic things like posture require the authority of a teacher. For Christians it should be axiomatic – but often it is not – that sound common sense is of divine inspiration!

The first essential in occult and yogic meditation is a correct and comfortable posture. The first consideration is not devotion, it is symmetry. Teachers such as Knight and Regardie suggest that, for the Western European, the best posture is for him to be seated on an upright chair, with legs and feet together, with a footrest if desirable for comfort, and with the spine erect. Knight is insistent that pains must be taken to make a comfortable position possible, and this involves experiment and preparation. Mouni Sadhu, an exponent of Yoga, makes similar suggestions for identical reasons. Knight describes occultism as 'the Yoga of the West', and this is an apt description, for there is little doubt that the modern occultist has learned a good many 'tricks of the trade' from his Eastern brother.

A comfortable, sitting posture, with the weight hanging from the ribs (as one writer puts it) is the first beginning. The occult student is then taught the necessity of making a deliberate gesture of 'switching on' which might be a movement of the hands as if drawing curtains apart. The suggestion is of 'opening the mysteries'. Knight, and the school to which he belongs, would then sign themselves with the cross. The invocation is not what we might expect; it is not the invocation of the Holy Trinity but the doxology of the Lord's Prayer of which Dion Fortune claimed, 'the man who wrote that knew his Qabalah!'

The gesture is made as follows: forehead, breast, right shoulder, left shoulder. The hands are then clasped on the breast. The invocation is: 'For thine is the Kingdom (Malkuth), the Power (Geburah) and the Glory (Gedulah, Chesed).' The Hebrew text is preferred. The significance of the gesture is now clear; it is a tracing of a part of the Tree of Life on the body, and *not* the Cross of Christ.

The opening and dedicatory gestures having been made, the symmetrical posture is resumed. These gestures are important, they have a real and valid psychological purpose; they do in fact help to 'switch on' and their effect is more profound than is often realized. Subjective though they are, they express to the conscious (and subconscious) mind of the person making them the idea of a *clean break*, and this is important. Christians are also accustomed to the idea of small, usually private, gestures and rituals at the commencement of prayer. The commonest of these is the sign of the cross and the invocation of the Holy Trinity. The lighting of a candle is another, and a profounder gesture than most realize who prefer to misunderstand its significance!

The next important step is a thorough and systematic relaxation of the muscles, beginning at the head and consciously working down to the feet. This takes time to master, sometimes more than five minutes at first. Young mothers-to-be are taught an almost identical technique. For them it is very important; for the meditator it is no less important. Recollection is prevented and disrupted not only actually but perfectly validly by the protest of an over-tense muscle, by a foot 'gone to sleep', by 'pins and needles' and by a thousand other lamentably unspiritual things. The body, if it is to play its part, must be given due consideration. The Christian must not neglect 'Brother Ass'. He too is in Christ.

The relaxation of muscles is followed by deep, rhythmical breathing. This is a habit that must be acquired because it is difficult to breathe deeply and rhythmically for any length of time without straining or 'puffing and blowing'. Once the habit is mastered it is a very deeply relaxing and quietening technique.

Breath itself has a long-standing semi-occult, semi-sacramental significance. A deliberately directed breath is often used in exorcism as a kind of 'outward sign'. Our Lord himself used a deliberate breath in a sacramental manner when he 'breathed on them, saying, "Receive the Holy Spirit",' (John xx. 22). The conscious direction of rhythmical breathing will be encountered again, but it is possibly worth remembering that, in certain degrees of mystical prayer, the function of breathing appears to be almost, if not entirely suspended! There is, however, a distinction which will shortly become apparent between occult meditation and mental prayer. The distinction is absolute, but no value judgements are intended in the making of it.

These preparations having been done, the student, in his early stages, will proceed with discursive meditation in a manner similar to that advocated by St Ignatius. Indeed, up to this point, the yogic and occult techniques are relevant and helpful to the Christian seeking entry into silent prayer. What is here described as a formal discipline is informally practised by many who seek to pray that way. Their recollection will not have been attained until the fundamental bodily requirements of relaxation, comfort, erect spine and relaxed and rhythmical breathing have been met. They will not, perhaps, have been conscious that they have met these requirements; no drill will have been performed, but the requirements are basic and must be met. The yogic and occult drill acknowledges the body and is not prey, as Christians sometimes are, to inhibitions about posture. It is worth remembering that the Holy Spirit came, at Pentecost, to the Church when it was *sitting!* (Acts ii. 2) Thus the Church is forever liberated from 'sacred postures'.

In the early stages of his instruction the student of occult meditation will be taught to bring his meditation to a close with a brief check on his relaxation and a conscious attention to his rhythmical breathing before rising to his feet and performing a 'closing sign' (closing the imaginary curtains) and signing himself with the Qabalistic cross. The final act of closure is a deliberate stamp of the foot and a conscious attention to surroundings.

This 'switching off drill' is very sensible indeed because it is more important than it may seem to make a clean break out of meditation. There is more that is undesirable about an unconcluded meditation than a tendency to day-dream. The student is instructed to make good use of pencil and paper, but *after* the meditation. He must note down his experience and all 'results', as much for his teacher's benefit as for his own. The pencil and paper find their way into some forms of Christian prayer and meditation, but *within* the meditation not outside it. This usage is one which some souls find helpful but probably not many. The student of the occult will be instructed to meditate at noon (if possible) and last thing at night, in bed. The good reason for the latter exercise is that, if sleep overtakes the student in the midst of his meditation, his unconscious mind will be working on profound and healthy matters during the hours of sleep. This is, in itself, a good thing.

The art of visualization is of the essence of occultism. In this respect there is an affinity between occult techniques and those of St Ignatius. The Saint, however, intended that the formal discursive, meditation should precede – indeed provoke – forty minutes colloquy in which the disciplined exercise of mind should give place to affective or contemplative prayer, the essence of which is not 'thought' but 'love'. The concern of the occultist is the raising of consciousness to higher (or perhaps deeper) levels; there is a very close resemblance between occult meditation and mental prayer. They are, however, two entirely distinct and separate exercises.

The first important exercise in visualization is known as 'building the middle pillar'. This exercise which is the main subject of Regardie's monograph, *The Art of True Healing*, consists of the construction, in the pictorial imagination, of the central pillar of the Tree of Life. The Sephirah Kether is visualized as a brilliant sphere emanating immediately above the head, and some time is spent holding this visualization in the mind. This is accompanied by a practice strange to the Christian but common in occultism; that of 'vibration'. The god-name of the Sephirah is vibrated, that is to say, the Hebrew word 'Eheieh' is chanted repetitively, over and over again. A rhythm is established which is considered to be the correct 'rhythm' of the Sephirah; the vibration is done aloud when circumstances permit, otherwise it may be done silently. The effect is, to some degree, a form of self-hypnosis, but it is held to be a powerful aid to concentration. Some slight resemblance may perhaps be found between occult vibration and the technique advocated by the author of the *Cloud of Unknowing* in which a word of one syllable is 'clung to', performing the function in the concentrating mind of 'cats-eyes' on a fog-bound road. The resemblance is, however, slight and superficial. The god-name is, in a sense, a Word of Power; the vibration of it is believed to *do something*. The vibration of the god-name has another function; it establishes the occultist's consciousness on the Sephirah at its highest level, in the world of Atziluth. He is always wary of failing to invoke the highest principle first as a counter to any danger from the demonic.

Perhaps it should be remembered that, important though the vibration of the god-name might be to an occultist; that strange and colourful magus, Crowley, claimed to have attained satisfactory results by vibrating – of all things – 'Greenland's Icy Mountains'!

From Kether, above the head, the student must then visualize the descent of a brilliant stream of light to the throat, where the mysterious Sephirah, Daath, is constructed in the imagination, and its god-name vibrated. In due time – and over the course of many sessions – Tiphareth is constructed over the heart, Yesod over the loins, and Malkuth at the feet. The 'middle pillar' is then complete, and the construction of the middle pillar now becomes an *additional preliminary* to meditation when the student has mastered its visualization.

It is perhaps to be expected that the next exercise concerns the visualization of the remaining Sephiroth, situated as follows: on the left side of the head – Chokmah; on the left shoulder – Chesed; on the left hip – Netzach. On the right side of the head – Binah; on the right shoulder – Geburah; on the right hip – Hod. To this visualization is added a new breathing exercise called 'the fountain' in which the breath is drawn down to below the breast and visualized as ejected, on the exhale, as a fountain from the top of the head, flowing down to the feet, covering the whole tree that has been built.

In this, and in other, related exercises, there appears to be a connection with the yogic exercise of constructing what is known as 'odic armour', and which resembles nothing so much as a visualization of the egg-shaped 'membrane' in Dr Assagioli's diagram. The yogic exercise 'armours' this imaginary membrane to make it proof against attack. These things are not mere flights of fancy; there is indeed an 'armour' which is supplied by recollection. Attack via the collective unconscious is a feature of much primitive witchcraft and is practised to this day in parts of Africa and among Australian aborigines. The direction of concentrated raw emotion against a 'target' was the function of the Celtic magician and an adequate 'counter-magic' could bounce it back upon himself! Sophistication must not blind us to matters which modern psychology is beginning to rediscover, and of which prayerful people are aware without constructing vocabularies or systems to articulate their awareness. We must not forget that the incarnation was an incarnation involving the unconscious as well as the conscious. The principle of redemption operates within the collective unconscious; this is the principle behind both exorcism and spiritual healing.

This process of relaxation, breathing and visualization might seem to be dreadfully complicated to the newcomer. In fact, there is a considerable unity and simplicity about it all. The difficulty is, of course, the training in concentration. The middle pillar, and indeed the whole tree, are visualized in white light at the beginning of the exercise, but slowly, Sephirah by Sephirah, the principle of colour is introduced. Colours are arranged, by the occultist, in four 'scales'. These scales each relate to the four 'worlds' and the operative principles of those worlds in each Sephirah. Briefly, the matter may be tabulated as follows; the details of the colours in each scale for each Sephirah may be found in the appendix to part two of this work.

In the case of each Sephirah, therefore:

World	Colour Scale	Operative Principle
Atziluth	King Scale	God-name
Briah	Queen Scale	Archangel
Yetzirah	Emperor Scale	Order of Angels
Assiah	Empress Scale	Mundane Chakra

There is much to be learned by heart, but it ties together remarkably neatly.

The discipline of learning to build up in the pictorial imagination the Tree of Life in its correct colours in any given scale as a preliminary to any actual meditation – *before, in other words, the experience for which the occultist yearns can even be sought* – reveals serious occultism to be both disciplined and demanding to a high degree. The whole purpose of this exercise is to train the student to know and to handle his basic 'weapons', the symbols with which he will seek to probe the unconscious levels. Untrained and unsure, he will speedily be both deluded and dismayed. The seeker after 'instant experience' will never last out this course; he will drift into tinkering in 'black magic', or he will take mescaline or LSD.

It will be worth our while to lay occultism aside for a moment and briefly examine its Eastern equivalent, Yoga. Mouni Sadhu, in his book, *Concentration*, deals in succession with the self-same basic matters that we have discussed. He too suggests an unupholstered upright chair, relaxation, and rhythmical breathing (Asana and Pranayama), His teaching is close to that of Knight, but the principle of colour is introduced somewhat differently, in the context of rhythmical breathing. 'Sit in your usual posture and imagine the whole of surrounding space to be filled with a bright (never dark) ocean of the required colour. Something like being in an immaterial, crystal-clear coloured fluid. Imagine that you are drawing it in through your nostrils when inhaling and allowing it to emerge again as you exhale. That is *all* that is needed for our purpose.'[1] There is, behind this, the conviction that colours, when visualized, subtly influence what in yogic and occult language is described as the 'astro-mental perceptions'. Mouni Sadhu gives a table of colours and their attributes which is briefly rendered as follows:

Rose-red Uplifts the energies, stimulates wakefulness, dispels sleepiness, etc. (A warning is given about avoiding dark shades of this colour.)
Orange Stimulates and purifies.
Green Aids relaxation, eases tensions, anxieties, etc.
Blue Similar to green but not so suitable for Pranayama (breathing).
Yellow Similar to orange, but subtler in effect.
Violet Purifying and uplifting. Stimulates inner detachment.
White Synthesis of all colours. To be used in advanced exercises only, aimed at the attainment of Samadhi (superconsciousness).

The occultist will hasten to relate this table to his own, and we shall not argue with him. We shall, however, take note of the correspondences which may be observed between this table and the philosophy behind advertising techniques and interior decoration. It is an interesting exercise to match the colours of the Church's Liturgical Year with Mouni Sadhu's table!

It is now necessary to outline a few further exercises which the occult student will attempt before he begins the 'path-working' which is the real essence of this discipline. Most interesting is perhaps an essay in self-examination against the Qliphothic (demonic) attributes of the Sephiroth – in other words their associated vices. He meditates upon the vices of the Sephiroth in turn, asking himself in what respect does he mirror them in his own personality. This exercise is known as the construction of the 'black magic mirror'. This is followed by a meditation upon the virtues associated with the Sephiroth – the 'white magic mirror'. The student is expected to be brutally frank with himself. Self-knowledge is regarded as of absolute importance, and every effort is made to arrive at it.

A flexing of his visualizing muscles (if such an expression may be permitted) is performed by the systematic concentration upon one Sephirah, while at the same time holding the others present but in the 'shadows' of the pictorial imagination. In Yoga and in occultism, concentration is vital; the exercises of the latter are more varied, more colourful, more interesting, than the brutal, bare simplicity of the former. The 'Yoga of the West' is, in fact, Western and approaches the Western mind realistically. When the time comes for a beginning of path-working, to these preliminaries is added what is called a 'Mantram', a form of words intended to affect and focus the consciousness on the desired subject.

These, then, are the preliminary techniques which must be mastered by the student of occultism before he can safely begin the investigation of the unconscious by the use of symbols. The question may be asked, 'Is such a venture ever safe?' Another questioner will ask 'Is such a venture lawful?' The first question is real, and the answer is probably no. The second implies pre-judgement of the issue. The most important question that must be asked at this stage is 'What is the nature of such an exercise?' in other words, is it broadly 'religious', or is it rather 'scientific'?

Here is the confusion. Here is where clarity must be found, and that is no easy matter.

References

1   Mouni Sadhu, *Concentration*, George Allen & Unwin, pp. 82-5

Paths and Path-Working

'MAGIC, as already remarked, is a practical system; claims Israel Regardie, 'and every part has been devised for experiment ... we ask for experiment; demand it even, for the sake of mankind. We invite the earnest and sincere student to experiment for himself with that technique described in Chapter Ten of my book *The Tree of Life*, and then compare his results, the journey to anyone path or Sephirah, with the correspondences briefly delineated in my other work *A Garden of Pomegranates* or in Dion Fortune's book *The Mystical Qabalah*. It is with the utmost confidence that I say one hundred astral journeys obtained in that way will correspond in *every* instance with the major symbols, names, numbers and ideas recorded in the several books of the Qabalah.'[1]

We must ask ourselves the question, 'What is this statement, made so confidently? Is it a statement in respect of religious experience, or is it a statement in respect of scientific observation? Is it, in some sense, in respect of both?' Having asked that question, we shall be careful to avoid answering it prematurely; the question is too important for that. We shall keep it in the back of our minds as we go on.

When we examined the objective Qabalah, the ten Sephiroth, we began at Kether and followed the Sephiroth in sequence of emanation until we arrived at Malkuth. Path-working is performed in the opposite direction. Man, the microcosm, must begin where he is in the physical world and work upwards to the light. There is more to this than simply proceeding: Makuth – Yesod (thirty-second path); Yesod – Tiphareth (twenty-fifth path), and Tiphareth – Daath – Kether (thirteenth path). This is the basic direction, but the consciousness must tread all twenty-two paths of the subjective Qabalah if it is to complete the great work. Of this first path, the thirty-second on the tree, Knight writes:

> 'This path joins Malkuth, the physical world, and Yesod, the universal unconscious and etheric web which forms the foundation of physical existence. It is therefore a path of introversion from the sensory consciousness to the consciousness of the deeps of the inner world. When one treads it one is boring down into the unconscious mind and many and strange are the things that one may meet there. It is like the hole in the earth into which

Alice fell, leading to her strange adventures in Wonderland. It is also, on a mythological level, the way down to the Underworld, trod by Oedipus at Colonos, Orpheus in search of Eurydice and many others; but primarily it is Persephone's descent into the world of Pluto, the King of the Underworld. Alice, indeed, might be said to be a modern version of Persephone, for Carroll was a writer who wrote of the deeps of the unconscious mind.'[2]

This important passage introduces an important principle, that of pagan mythology. The symbolism of pagan mythology is very profound and a favourite method of path-working is by means of meditation on pagan myths and symbols.

We shall examine an example of this kind of thing in due course, but for the moment, let us allow Knight to continue.

'The path is also the way of psycho-analysis and shows the difference between the Freudian and Jungian techniques, for when the unconscious images of Yesod are met with the Freudian tries to analyse them with reference to life history in Malkuth, daily living, but the Jungian process follows the images through until they become symbols of transformation leading to the psychic harmony of Tiphareth. In other words, the Jungian technique is, or should be, a pressing on to the twenty-fifth path, Yesod–Tiphareth, after the way in, the thirty-second path, Malkuth–Yesod, has been trodden.'[3]

It will be helpful, at this point, to discover just what is meant by a meditation on symbols. Here we are fortunate in that the teacher and writer on occultism, Israel Regardie, has recorded a particularly vivid example of a journey on the thirty-second path and the arrival at Yesod. It is worth our while to hear him at length.

'Let me quote from the record of a colleague an illuminating passage or two illustrating what I mean. The following is a "vision" or waking dream – fantasy of the so-called thirty-second path. "We marched down the wide indigo road. There was a cloudy night-sky – no stars. The road was raised above the general level of the ground. There was a canal each side beyond which we could see the lights of what appeared to be a large city. We went on like this for a long way, but then I noticed in the distance a tiny figure of a woman, like a miniature – she seemed to be naked, but as she drew near, I saw a scarf floating round her. She had a crown of stars on her head and in her hands were two wands. She came towards us very quickly, and I gazed fascinatedly at a string of pearls reaching from her neck to her knees – and gazing, found that we had passed through the circle of her pearls, and she had disappeared!"'[4]

Regardie draws our attention to certain points in this narrative. The girl described is to be found exactly as described on the tarot trump XXI, the trump assigned to this path. The colour of the road – indigo – is the colour assigned to the path, and the surrounding night suggests the blue-black alternative colour. But let Regardie continue: 'I must pass on to a brief description of the entrance to Yesod. "Now the sky is clear and full of stars ... The moon, a great yellow harvest moon, rises slowly up the sky to a full arch ... and we saw the moon shining on the high purple walls of a city ... We did not delay to look about, but marched quickly to the centre of the city, to an open space, in the midst of which was a round temple like a ball of silver. It was approached by nine steps, and rested on a silver platform. It had four doors. Before each was a large angel with silver wings ... Inside, we were in a very airy place. Light breezes lifted our clothes and our hair – the interior was very white and clear silvery – no colours. Suspended in the centre was a great globe, like the moon itself. ... While we looked we saw that the globe was not suspended in the air; it rested on immense cupped hands. We followed the arms up and saw, far up near the roof, deep dark eyes looking down, dark like the night sky. And a voice said ..." Little point would be gained to continue with the rest of the quotation. This passage is given here solely that the reader may refer to the description of the astral plane in the textbooks, and then to the recurrence in this vision of the major symbols, and the dynamic form of dramatization.'[5]

Regardie goes on to prove his point by examining the symbols revealed. 'Let the student take good notice of the presence of the correct numbers, colours, planetary attributions, and above all the hint as to how much valuable knowledge may be acquired. Note the four doors to the Temple representing the four major elements of fire, water, air and earth. For this astral world is also referred to the ether (of which the element air is a surrogate), the fifth element, quintessentializing the lower elements, the temple to which the other elements are but doors. Suspended in the centre of the temple was a globe, symbolic possibly of the air itself which, in the Hindu Tattwa system, is represented by a blue sphere. Before each of the doors stands an angel. These are the four Kerubic angels, the vice-regents of the four cardinal quarters and elements, ruling over a particular elemental world under the dominance of one of the letters of the Tetragrammaton. Possibly they are representations of the interior psychic delimitation of the soul's spatial area, so to speak, the absence of which would indicate an unhealthy diffusion or decentralization of consciousness. Also the four cardinal points of space would be represented by these four angelic figures –

concretizations, too, of the double play of the moral opposites. East is opposite to west, and north opposite to south, whilst each of these quarters has attributed to it some particular moral quality or psychic function. The sense of being in an airy place with light breezes bears out the formal attribution of air – a curious confirmation of the duality of meaning implied in *pneuma*, wind and spirit, a duality which occurs not only in the Greek, but in Hebrew, Arabic, and a host of primitive languages.' [6]

The sceptic will approach this description of the thirty-second path and the arrival at Yesod with a number of awkward questions. Granted that this is a deliberate dramatization, the normal mode of operation of the pictorial imagination (compare St Ignatius), is it not highly probable, he will ask, that the student, exhaustively drilled in the symbolism before he ever begins, will faithfully reproduce the correct symbolism in his meditation, consciously or unconsciously? This a very awkward question for the occultist to answer; the probable – honest answer would be, 'he might, or he might not'. The occultist would claim a virtually identical symbol pattern reproduced by, not one, but very many students. He would claim as much right to build a hypothesis on this as that granted to Freud and Jung in a not dissimilar exercise – the analysis of dreams. The sceptic might or might not concede this point, but the Christian would be asking himself another question while the argument was in progress. 'Fascinating,' he would say, 'but so what?'

A reference has been made, in the foregoing paragraph, to two most distinguished pioneers of psychotherapy. It will be very much worth our while to depart from the occult for the moment, and join the psychotherapists.

Assagioli, in the chapter on his book devoted to techniques of personal psychosynthesis, makes extensive mention of the use of symbols, both as an aid to diagnosis and as a form of treatment. There is mention of comfortable posture, relaxation, rhythmical breathing, visualization of certain sets of circumstances, ideal patterns, and so forth, ending with a deliberate exercise of the patient's will. Symbols, he claims, have three main functions.

'Their primitive and basic dynamic function is that of being accumulators, in the electrical sense, as containers and preservers of a dynamic psychological charge or voltage. Their second function, a most important one, is that of transformers of psychological energies. A third function is that of conductors or channels of psychological energies. From the qualitative point of view symbols can be considered as images of psychological realities of many kinds.' [7]

Among many suggested usages of symbol there is included a presentation of symbols to the patient from a selection divided into seven categories. These are, briefly, nature symbols, animal symbols, human symbols, man-made symbols, religious and mythological symbols, abstract symbols and individual or spontaneous symbols. 'How do we present these different symbols to the patient?' he asks; 'there are three main ways: firstly, by simply naming the symbol or giving a short description of it; secondly, by observation, i.e. presenting to the patient a drawing or image of the symbol in question; and, thirdly, by visualization, i.e. asking the patient to visualize, evoke an inner image of the symbol. This latter procedure is needed for dynamic symbols, i.e. for symbols of action, which undergo transformation and pass through different stages.'[8] The procedure for the utilization of symbols he divides into three ways:

1. Presenting, offering, or suggesting the use of a definite symbol out of the first six classes or groups of symbols.
2. Fostering, or taking advantage of the appearance of spontaneous symbols in the course of treatment, a procedure which was widely used by Jung.
3. An intermediate way, that used by Desoille, who in his method ... first suggests a symbol, mainly that of ascending and of descending, and then lets the patient develop freely his own subsidiary symbols. This method, used ably as Desoille does, can give very good therapeutic results. [9]

Already, we can discern a link between occult meditation and psychotherapeutic 'meditation', both in method and matter. We shall follow this correspondence further, both in this chapter and in the chapter to follow. Immediately before the section of his book to which we must next attend, however, there is a reference to the psychological effects upon the individual of colour. 'It is now generally accepted that so-called "cold" and subdued colours have a quieting effect, and that "warm", vivid and bright colours have a stimulating or exciting influence. Certain shades of blue are usually considered as having a soothing, harmonizing effect; light green is refreshing; red and bright yellow are usually stimulating, while pink suggests serenity and happiness.' [10] It is an enlightening exercise to compare Assagioli with Mouni Sadhu in the foregoing chapter.

'Initiated symbol projection (ISP) is both a psycho-diagnostic and psycho-therapeutic technique. ... Developed in West Germany since 1948 largely as a therapy, only more recently have standard diagnostic procedures been established, based on clinical success.'[11] Assagioli's chapter on ISP is a resume of the work of three therapists, Happich,

Leuner and Desoille, who employ a most interesting system of symbol-meditation based on twelve basic symbols.

The first symbol is that of *a meadow*. This serves as a kind of psychological 'Garden of Eden', a beginning of psychological development during which something 'went wrong'. This symbol is readily accepted by both adults and children; it suggests a return to nature and a fresh beginning. Often the patients will describe a meadow with which they are familiar, but they are encouraged to 'walk on' until they encounter a part of the meadow which they have never seen in this world, into which they can project more freely. Difficulties are overcome by the suggestion, by the therapist, of length of grass, warmness of sun and so forth. The patient's own visualizations of such things give a fair indication of his 'general psychological health'. Some patients, for example, are so alienated from their own inner life that they can visualize only a desert. The appropriate 'symbol-therapy' would be a suggestion that the desert be 'watered' so that grass might grow.

The second symbol is that of *a mountain*. The level of aspiration of the patient is fairly clearly indicated by his description of the mountain and his efforts to climb it. Obstacles blocking the path are good indicators of the nature of inner hindrances. The third symbol is a *following of the course of a stream*. The amount of water is an indication of the total psychic energy (libido) flowing through the subject's psychic structure. The depth and breadth of the stream appear to correspond to the common descriptions of persons as 'deep', 'shallow', 'broad-minded' or 'narrow'! Obstacles and turbulences are symbolic expressions of conflicts, complexes and so forth. Clarity or cloudiness of the water indicate something of the patient's awareness of what is going on 'under the surface'.

The visualization of *a house* as a symbol of the subject's self (with discovery of hitherto unknown 'rooms', etc.); the description of the *ideal personality*, and the investigation of unconscious affective relationships *under the symbols of animals* follow from the first. In the latter, the mother and father of the patient are pictured (in the 'meadow') as a cow and a bull respectively, and their 'behaviour' and 'attitude' described under that symbol.

Unconscious attitudes towards sexuality are probed, in the case of males, by the visualization of roses in a rose-garden. In the case of females, by the visualization of the woman herself walking home in the dark and being offered a lift by a passing car. The colour and size of the car, the sex and appearance of the driver have considerable significance. Most significant are signs of resistance such as the ability to visualize the road, but not the car; or the disappearance of the car on the woman entering it.

A pool of water in a swamp often discloses a fearsome monster, or else a naked figure of the opposite sex, sexually threatening (in the case of women patients), or etherial (in the case of men). A similar exercise is *waiting for a figure to emerge from a cave.* The *eruption of a volcano* is a good index of the nature and amount of affective tension stored up within the patient. A *lion* will indicate the patient's ability to cope with his real life opponents, and an *old picture book* will often reveal matters that the previous visualization exercises have passed over.[12]

There is now little doubt about the connection between the technique of the occultist and that of the psychotherapist. This connection will become even more apparent in the chapter which follows. The sceptic will ask many awkward questions which will be answered by references to cases and empirical observations verified and counter-checked. The psychotherapist must remain a sceptic and a persistent questioner himself. The Christian will not ask his own awkward question, 'So what?' (He might be either therapist or patient in this case!) It will not be a relevant question in this context.

It will be worth our while to begin pondering the significance of the fact that the question, 'So what?' appears to the Christian to be relevant to a technique practised by the occultist on the one hand, but not to an essentially similar technique practised by the psychotherapist on the other. Why?

References

1   Israel Regardie, *The Art and Meaning of Magic*, Helios, p. 90
2   Knight, Vol. II, p. 1
3   Knight, Vol. II, pp. 1-2
4   Regardie, pp. 21-2
5   Regardie, pp. 22-5
6   Regardie, p. 25
7   Assagioli, pp. 177-8
8   Assagioli, p. 185
9   Assagioli, pp. 180-1
10 Assagioli, p. 285
11 Assagioli, p. 287
12 Assagioli, pp. 294-8

High Quests and Holy Grails

GROUP meditation is not a recognized feature of Christian devotion. The corporate action of the Body of Christ is the Eucharist; this expresses what the Church essentially is, and also what its individual members are. It is essentially a corporate act, an act of Christ-in-his-Body, through and in his members. An extension of this act is the Daily Office, the *Opus Dei*. This too is essentially a corporate act. Beyond the Eucharist and its extension, the Office, the devotional life of the Church is primarily individual; the individual devotions being summed up in the objective expression of the fact of the Christ which is the Eucharist.

Religious communities frequently fix a time on the timetable for silent prayer, but although all may perform this in one place and at one time, it is nevertheless a time of individual devotion. Others who follow the way of silent prayer occasionally do so in the company of other worshippers, but this is simply a matter of convenience or preference. The devotion of the Christian, outside the Eucharist, is mostly, but not entirely, his own individual concern. The concept of the 'concentration of minds' does not apply. It is love that is in play, not mind. Prayer is an exercise of will; the self-surrender of the will to God in love.

Corporate meditation is, however, a feature of both occultism and psychotherapy. There is claimed by both schools an enhancement of the whole enterprise by the linkage of minds on a common object, via the unconscious. This idea is at the root of the concept of 'Noosphere' developed by Teilhard de Chardin, who sees the growing together of mankind on the level of mind to be a tangible sign of the coming unification of all things culminating in what he calls 'Omega'.

There is no reason to doubt that two minds, or more, are more receptive working together than working independently. The psychic are certainly aware of this; an automatic, sceptical denial of this is pointless. We shall therefore examine, in outline, a method of occult meditation, which may be used either individually or corporately, which employs as its symbol structure the Arthurian Legends.

The most favoured method of pictorial meditation is by mythological visualization. The pagan pantheons supply a rich symbolism and, being themselves the expressions of the collective unconscious, they may be expected to prove reliable guides to the depths which are to be explored. The Arthurian legends are particularly valuable in that they are the product of a 'national' section of the corporate mind, over many centuries. The Englishman, or the Welshman, can become attuned to the idea of Arthur and all the associated symbols very easily. There is not the rather unreal 'draped female and Grecian urn' atmosphere which might attend an English excursion into Hellenic mysteries. We know where we are with Camelot (or we think we do). Bearing in mind the extensive preliminaries which we have studied, the construction of the Tree and the visualization of it, the construction of the occult version of the yogic 'odic armour' and every other psychological – or magical – preparation, let us now outline the course of a 'middle pillar' path-working using the Arthurian legend and the idea of the holy grail.

King Arthur – a King is the magical image of the Sephirah Tiphareth, the centre of harmony, the 'Christ centre'. The intention of this and all exercises in magical meditation is self-knowledge, the discovery of the true self; and the spiritual experience of Tiphareth is, in one description, the 'knowledge and conversation of the Holy Guardian Angel' – the discovery of the true self. Relating this to Assagioli's diagram (a thing he never intended) we are seeking to penetrate the higher unconscious and arrive at the true self; perfect integration of the personality. This is an exercise up the 'middle pillar' from Malkuth to Tiphareth.

The preliminaries having been performed, the student concentrates upon the Sephirah Tiphareth as subjectively situated in the region of his heart. From this he 'projects' a 'round table' expanding it from a point of light to a diameter of about six inches (in the imagination). The table is then furnished. It is of indigo colour and there are twelve golden lines radiating from the centre dividing the table into the twelve segments of the zodiac. In the centre of the table, standing in a circle, and covered by a transparent veil, is a golden chalice, symbol of refreshment. At each place at table is found a small silver chalice engraved with a zodical sign. (These may be replaced by either a lamp – symbol of counsel, or a sword – symbol of action.) The table having been constructed and furnished, it is expanded in the imagination until it is large enough to sit at.

This is the first exercise of visualization. At this early stage, a golden ray is visualized in the mind's eye, striking down from Tiphareth into the chalice. The subject for meditation, or the problem to be solved, is then brooded upon in the confidence that some esoteric illumination will be received. When the exercise is completed, the table is deliberately diminished, withdrawn into the heart, and a deliberate break made. Notebook and pencil are then set to work.

The student of Jungian psychology will by now have recognized that the table is what is known as a 'mandala'. The circle appears to be a universal symbol of wholeness. The grail itself is a symbol of the wholeness for which man is ever searching; its quest is a kind of conferring of the benefits of the Blessed Sacrament in Arthurian and Parsifal legend. Rightly perceived, the Grail romances are a kind of poetic accompaniment to the chivalry of old Christendom of which Logres is an archetype.

The symbolism is so deep, however, that mystification and esoteric speculation are never far away. The Mandala is discovered again in the very Hall in which the table is found: the square – the quadrangular form generally – is a symbol of inner wholeness consciously perceived. In this connection, the determined attempts of popular devotion to enthrone Mary alongside the Holy Trinity – thus making a kind of Holy Quaternity – represent an expression of the urge for wholeness; in this case, fulfilling too prematurely the final consummation of all things, the marriage of the 'lamb' with the 'mystical bride'. In time, in the Christian revelation, the 'symbolic tension' must remain!

As proficiency in this new exercise in visualization is attained, the awareness is alerted to the 'brethren' at other 'sieges' round the table, each with their own silver chalice engraved with their own zodiacal sign. The student takes his siege at that segment of the table marked with the sign under which he was born. The whole of this 'Arthurian' system is built up slowly, detail by detail, until the whole can be brought into the mind's eye complete, at every session. Gradually, the 'brethren' are contacted, and the Sephiroth are meditated upon while seated at the 'siege'; 'the power of the chalice' conveying the 'Christ-force' is an important factor and a period of self-examination is expected of the student in the power of it.

The great hall and the table with its golden grail having been mastered by the powers of visualization, the student then explores the castle, and in due time, ventures beyond its walls to the streets of Camelot, to the cottages of 'wise men' and so forth. The symbolism and the *colours* are carefully controlled.

Let a description of the 'chapel' suffice. It is situated to the East of the great hall, reached via a square-headed door before which hangs a golden curtain. A short, narrow passage leads to a small chapel built of grey stone, in the centre of which stands a cubical altar on a platform of three steps. A Celtic Cross is on the altar with, at its centre, a rose. A thick mauve carpet is on the floor and a great sword lies on the altar – Excalibur. The cube and the rose-cross are symbols of Tiphareth, the remaining symbols are carefully thought-out too.

This description (for which I am grateful to Gareth Knight) is vivid and fascinating. The question still persists, however, 'in the end – so what?' What *is* the end? This is the problem.

We cannot, however, dismiss this style of meditation lightly as a fascinating but esoteric form of fantasy-making. The sceptic who would take this view will be taken aback by the discovery that the psychotherapist uses an almost identical technique in 'group meditation' on – believe it or not – the grail legends! The example that we shall examine uses the continental legends, those of Titurel and Parsifal. There is a 'castle' and a 'temple'; there are 'knights' – there is, in fact, the whole colourful and elaborate set-up, all with the intention of awakening the patient to self-realization and bringing out latent qualities. The example that follows comes from the chapter in Assagioli's book dealing with spiritual psychosynthesis.

'This exercise,' writes Assagioli, 'can be done by an individual alone, but it is particularly effective as a group exercise for intra-group psychosynthesis. We will therefore outline its use by a group. At each meeting – usually held weekly – the leader of the group or therapist describes the series of symbols, and their significance, to be found in the text of Wagner's operas *Lohengrin*, *Parsifal*, and the various books on the grail legend and the grail knights. Each time a symbol is described and its significance explained, passages of music by Wagner appropriate to the theme are played; following this the group is requested to think about and reflect upon the symbol in order to realize its significance. Each member is asked to introject the symbol, so to speak, to identify himself with it. For instance, at the first group meeting, the identification is with Titurel; and then subsequently with each of the characters in the succeeding symbolic scenes of the opera. ... It is suggested that the following series of symbols be presented during the group exercise:

1st week: Titurel as the symbol of a man who is dissatisfied under the worries of existence, and who therefore decides to leave the world with which he has been identified. He sets out to climb to the top of the mountain and persists with courage until he reaches the summit.'[1]

Assagioli elaborates on this as an exercise in leaving the centre of consciousness to travel – ascend – to higher levels seeking superconsciousness and the spiritual self.

2nd week: The watch in the night. Titurel spends the night in prayer on top of the mountain asking for inspiration. His kneeling under the sky is a symbol of invocation. Here we have the use of techniques of concentration, contemplation, invocation, and silence – the higher active introvertion.'

3rd week: 'The response to Titurel's invocation. A point of light appears in the sky, then a host of angels appears. During the presentation of this symbol to the group the prelude to *Lohengrin* may be played. An angel brings the cup (the grail of the legend, the symbol of love) and the spear (the symbol of power or will) ...'

4th week: The founding of the orders of the knights; Titurel finds and chooses his co-workers and creates the group. This is a symbol of inter-individual psychosynthesis. In co-operation the knights build the castle and the temple; and here again the castle represents the power aspect, and is a symbol of might, while the temple is the symbol of the religious aspect of love, the place of communion with the spirit.'

5th week: 'The life of the group of knights in the community which they have created; the successful functioning of the order, symbolizing group psychosynthesis, brotherhood, friendship, group co-operation.' [2]

Assagioli explains at this point that, in the opera, Titurel falls from grace through the temptations of Kundry, the tool of the evil magician Klingsor, and is thus unable to fulfil his duties as head of the order. This is not, however, part of the therapy!

6th week: The mission of the grail order in the world. The appeal by the men of the plains for help; the descent of the knights from the mountain into the plains for the selfless purpose of service to humanity ...The descent into the plains illustrates a very important principle of spiritual pychosynthesis: *viz.* that the realization of the spiritual self is not for the purpose of withdrawal but for the purpose of being able to perform more effective service in the world of men.' [3] In this, the principle met with earlier in this book, the responsible occultist's claim, 'I seek to know in order to serve' is echoed. It is the claim of the doctor and the scientist.

7th week: The knights, having performed their mission of service in the world, return to the castle and meet in their ritualistic ceremony. At the ceremony a white dove appears from above and the spear is seen hovering over the cup. This is symbolic of the recharging with spiritual energy, periodically needed for more efficient service. The grail knights commune as a group, and having been 'charged' for the future year of service they depart, leaving a nucleus who always remain in the castle and perform the duties of the community life there'.[4]

To the grail legend, Assagioli adds a similar exercise using the symbolism of Dante's *Divine Comedy*, and an exercise in visualising the blossoming of a rose – referring to the rose-cross which is the symbol of Tiphareth, but without, of course, mentioning that Sephirah or any other specifically Qabalistic concept. The Christian will recognize, in the grail-centred meditation of Assagioli, a kind of figure of the Christian, Eucharistically-centred life. This is the grand symbol of wholeness and the way to the true self. The portrayal is dramatic, poetic, and deliberately therapeutic in intention.

The similarities between the therapist's way and the occultist's are striking; but there is a difference. The occultist's meditation is a stage in the road from Malkuth to Kether – in other words, god with a small 'g' is winding himself up to a capital 'G'. The exaltation of the consciousness to the power infinity is the underlying intention. The Qabalist is careless of theology. Results are his requirement, and his theology is begged, borrowed and stolen from every point of the compass as long as it appears to be verifiable by results, by his experience. Thus a philosophical system from mediaeval Judaism, utterly transcendentalist in its origins, has been 'brilliantly misconceived' in Sholem's judgement and married to the monism and utter immanentism of Hinduism. The claim is made that the immanent and the transcendent are reconciled (see the first chapter of Part Two), but the 'monism' thus advanced is coming apart at the seams and will stand very little scholarly investigation.

The transcendent is, as it were, catered for, by the expedient of pushing the ultimate ever further and further away in the manner of the Gnostics. The resulting construction is in many respects brilliantly conceived and possessed of a validity of sorts – and perhaps considerable 'sorts' – as a kind of map of the 'within' of creation. It has an equal plausibility as a map of microcosmic man's 'within'. It falls into the total error, however, of equating creation in toto with God. Thus the occultist, while proceeding along a possibly promising path in terms of self-integration and the attainment of a deeper understanding of things, is deluded into supposing that he is in fact 'going to God' when he is doing nothing whatever of the sort.

In all fairness however, and in all truth, it must be said that Truth, the absolute is a unity. The scientist who is a Christian will undergo religious experiences because his empirical observations will reveal to him ever more and more of the glory of God. The occultist too will undergo religious experiences as his understanding and intuition deepen. God is not limited, and he will permit himself to be found by the sincere and devout soul seeking him with purity of heart in the best way known to it.

But occultism *as a religion* is a pre-Christian speculation, utterly and eternally obsolete. The best it can do is to arrive at the point at which nothing makes sense any more without the Incarnation. And the Incarnation is not *within* the closed-circuit of the Tree of Life. Our Lord's context is not the Sephirah Tiphareth, it is the totality of things, for in Christ, man – in whom the whole universe is mystically present – is 'taken up into God'.

All prefigurings, all symbols are fulfilled and transcended. All speculation fails before the ultimate and transcending fact of Christ who is eternally fully God, and fully man.

References

1   Assagioli, p. 208
2   Assagioli, pp. 208-9
3   Assagioli, p. 210
4   Assagioli, pp. 210-11

The Cloud of Unknowing

THIS is not a book of Christian apologetic, neither is it a textbook of Christian ascetic theology. Nevertheless it may help to preserve balance, and to avoid an impression that the Christian's approach to occult meditation is merely negative, if a very brief outline is given of the Christian way of mental prayer.

There are two traditions in Christendom, describing our knowledge of God. The first, the positive way, seeks to affirm what God is. The second, the negative way, seeks to say what He is not. The positive way describes God in terms of human attributes, raising them to the power infinity. This approach is Biblical and answers the criticism of it that God is being made in man's image by quoting holy writ to the effect that man is made in God's image and thus human virtues and graces are but a reflection of the divine attributes. This is the Way reflected in the Thomist 'five ways' of proving the existence of God. It is the way towards which Western minds are naturally inclined and it has dominated the Western Church, both Catholic and Protestant, for a thousand years.

The negative way, however, acknowledges that God is unknowable by the human intellect. The truths of religion can be grasped; the reality of God himself cannot. The mind can only become blank before a reality it can never assimilate. It is necessary therefore to 'unknow', to dismiss all pictures, images, intellectual propositions, and seek God in total 'darkness' – in what an unknown but profound mediaeval writer has called 'the cloud of unknowing'.

It will be seen at once that these two ways, the positive and the negative, are complementary, and it would not be too much to say that St Ignatius, in his insistence upon the very 'positive way' exercise of discursive and pictorial meditation, intended this to lead on to the increasingly 'negative way' exercises of affective prayer and contemplation. It is not always remembered by earnest advocates of the 'spiritual exercises' that the twenty minutes of discursive meditation were to *precede* forty minutes of colloquy.

Discursive, pictorial meditation is not in itself prayer, but it is intended, by St Ignatius, to *provoke* prayer. The awakening of the soul to the wonder and the love of God leads to affective prayer, an affectionate – and sometimes intensely affectionate – discourse between the soul and her heavenly bridegroom. This in turn, as it becomes more and more peaceful, and as the level of prayer becomes deeper, leads into contemplative prayer in which the whole intellect – indeed the whole being – enters into a 'fog', conscious only that this is the way to God and that only in darkness, and by 'emptying out' can ultimate light and fulfilment be achieved.

Contemplative prayer is probably the 'normal' way of prayer of the adult Christian at the present time. This statement can be easily misunderstood, however; the vast majority of adult Christians are, alas, untaught and ignorant about this way and are thus quite unaware that it is probably 'normal' for them. Many are quite unaware that the way in which their prayers are going is in fact prayer at all. It is a grave mistake to imagine that contemplation is the exclusive preserve of 'contemplatives'.

A very significant distinction between occult meditation and prayer is the fact that occult meditation can be done at will, as the will and the techniques are mastered, and 'results' may be expected with confidence; whereas Christian prayer, as often as not, obstinately refuses to yield any 'results' at all and every effort is expended in a desperate endeavour to attain the smallest trace of recollection. Five minutes conscious recollection in an hour of prayer is a good average for many people for most of the time. There are times, quite beyond human control, when recollection is immediate and prolonged and the prayer time manifestly blessed in every way. The 'norm' however is a barrage of distractions, a blistering aridity, and a determined, if somewhat embattled and precarious desire 'to want to want God'.

Christian prayer is a *dialogue of wills*. The time of prayer is a time of giving the undivided attention *of the will* to God. Often it is almost impossible to give the attention of the thoughts, but the will operates at a deeper level – the deepest level of all. It is the determination *to keep at it* that is paramount. 'Consolations', 'sweetnesses' and so forth are a matter of the profoundest delight when it is God's will that they be given, but the training of the will to want God *as he is in himself* and not as he is experienced by the senses is fundamental to the Christian way; fundamental indeed to salvation.

It is the opinion of the writer that nothing is likely to be more daunting to the occultist who seeks to become a Christian and to follow the Christian way of prayer than the utter lack of 'experience', the total absence of 'results' that is exceedingly likely to attend his attempts to pray. He will be tempted to imagine that he has done indeed what the Israelites feared they had done – left the fleshpots of Egypt to die of thirst in the desert. A positive conviction of the divine absence will weigh in on him, and only after he has resisted the temptation to return to the colours and the delights of occult meditation will he hear the voice that the Apostles heard on the Sea of Galilee in a different darkness; 'Be of good cheer: it is I; be not afraid' (Mark, vi. 50).

Quo Vadis?

THE twenty-fourth, twenty-fifth and twenty-sixth paths, Hod-Tiphareth, Yesod-Tiphareth and Netzach-Tiphareth respectively, are said by occultists to contain the experience which, in the language of St John of the Cross, is known as 'the dark night of the soul'. To be more precise, the purgation of the senses is the experience in question, also known as the 'dark night of the spirit'. The three ways in question are ways of wisdom, of devotional mysticism and of nature mysticism and art respectively. Of the middle path, Knight has this to say:

'This path, leading from Yesod to Tiphareth, is the direct line of contact between the individuality and personality and on it are developed the first glimmerings of mystical or higher consciousness. Before mystical consciousness can gain a hold in the lower vehicles, however, these vehicles have to be quietened and this process is symbolized by likening the process of development to a journey through a desert or wilderness, when the soul is thrown *entirely upon its own resources* [my italics], assisted only by Faith.'⁴ He makes reference to the dark night, and continues, 'in the symbolism of the twenty-fifth path the soul has to advance on the desert way, leaving behind the life of the outer and lower worlds, not yet conscious of the life of the inner and higher worlds, invoking the inner light that will become a golden dawn in the darkness'.²

We are presented with a problem which is at first perplexing. The quotations which Knight uses from St John of the Cross are apt; the symbolism is not hard to reconcile with that of the appropriate parts of the tree. Again, the correspondence between the diagrammatic representations of the tree on one hand and Dr Assagioli on the other are undeniable (although the doctor was insistent that his was a useful thumb-nail sketch and no more). It is very easy to imagine, with the Qabalist, that the middle pillar is a kind of diagrammatical representation of what spiritual writers have called the 'ladder of ascent'.

And yet, it just will not do. The Christian life of prayer simply refuses to fit into the picture. St John may be quoted most plausibly in descriptions of the twenty-fifth path, and also the thirteenth path (Tiphareth-Kether); but this was not what he was writing about! Something is wrong; but what?

Christian prayer does not proceed *through* what we may call the 'within' of creation to a God who is at the bottom of it (or at the top). God is not that kind of 'ground of our being' – in Tillich's well-worn phrase – who has emanated *his own self* as creation. *The Christian is not in the least concerned with uniting his Atman with the world-soul Brahman.* That union is, and forever has been. The prayer of the Christian starts *from within the uncreated.* The Christian prays in and through the Christ of whom he is made part by his baptism. The prayer of the Christian is caught up into the life of adoration of the Holy Trinity. By the Incarnation, our Lord became 'Perfect God and perfect man ... one, not by conversion of the Godhead into flesh, *but by taking of the manhood into God.*' As the Christian grows in grace, his prayer in and through Christ becomes more and more Christ's prayer *through him.* He lives, and yet – as St Paul reminds us, it is not himself but Christ who lives in him. This growth in grace continues until the unitive life begins in which the two, the lover and the loved, are one life of adoration. The Christian's prayer does not reach from Malkuth to Kether; it begins in Christ and grows 'into the measure of the stature of the fulness of Christ'. The Tree of Life has nothing whatever to do with it.

What therefore is the reason for the apparent correspondence between the 'ladder of ascent' and the 'middle pillar'? The reason is plain; the Tree of Life is a pattern of archetypal symbols and as such it is a 'map' of the 'within' of creation. Its accuracy is a matter for conjecture, but it represents at least a working hypothesis. The way of Christian prayer is echoed and shadowed upon it in ways which are, predictably, appropriate. Of course the symbolism 'fits'; man, although he is taken into God in Christ – and that is a 'potential' that is realised by Grace – is nevertheless *a created being;* indeed he is rightly understood as being *the emergent rational, moral consciousness of creation!* Knight has used a treatise on the real to illustrate the echo!

The true difference between the Qabalistic twenty-fifth path (and its flanking pair) and the dark night of the spirit can be better perceived by relating it to that other traditional Christian teaching on the same subject, that which speaks of the purgative and the illuminative ways. These somewhat less evocative terms better illustrate the *moral* significance of the realities with which they deal. 'The soul herself must be educated, must be purified and cleansed so perfectly as to be united with Christ by nothing except his grace,' writes R. H. Benson. 'She must be first purged and then illuminated, first stripped of herself and then adorned with his favours, before she is fit for her final union. These two stages are named by spiritual writers, the Way of Purgation and the Way of Illumination respectively.'[3] Benson makes it clear that there is a necessary element of destruction in every cleansing operation. He speaks of the great pleasure that the soul takes in all the external things which seem to be sanctified by Christ's presence; they seem to be in themselves 'heavenly and divine!' But he warns, 'extremely often, the first sign that the Way of Purgation has been really entered lies in a consciousness that there is beginning for her an experience which the world calls *disillusionment*.'[4] Benson suggests various catastrophes such as a disunited congregation, a spoiled priest, or, in respect of worship, 'the novelty begins to wear off'.

The world is full of wandering souls who have mistaken human romance for inner love, but the second stage in purgation is a disillusionment with divine things – the monotony of piety! 'There comes a time sooner or later when not only do the external things of religion – music, art, liturgy – ... begin to wear thin; but the very heart and essence of them begin to fail also. For example the actual exercise of prayer becomes wearisome ... the sacraments ... become wearisome and monotonous, and so far as she can see, do not fulfil their own promise ... Christ has cheated her, it almost seems, with promises he cannot or will not fulfil.'[5] This stage is one of great danger and many are the souls who wander away, either to some other religion which offers profitable and speedy returns in spiritual things, or to a kind of disillusioned sorrow that, after all, it 'did not work'. They have refused to learn the lesson of this stage, that the soul should serve God, and not God serve the soul!

The third stage is a deeper disillusionment still. It is a total disillusionment with self! 'She begins in this third stage to learn her own ignorance and her own sin, and to learn, too, that which ought to have been wholly incompatible with her ignorance and her sin – her amazing self-centredness and complacency. Up to now she has thought to possess Christ, to hold him as a lover and a friend, to grasp him and to keep him. Her previous mistakes came from this very thing; now she has to learn that not only must she relinquish all that is not Christ, but she *must relinquish Christ*. Leave, that is to say, her energetic hold on Him, and be content, instead, to be altogether held and supported by him ... she sees for the first time that there is no good in herself apart from Christ; that he must be all, and she nothing ... no longer can pride, whether whole or wounded, keep her from him for her pride at last is not wounded, but dead.'[6]

The gulf between occult meditation and Christian prayer, between the 'great work' and the way of abnegation, is absolute. The one – at best – strives 'back to OM'. The other is the only way 'on to OMEGA'. Whoever would be a Christian be he occultist or anything else, must burn his books and, in the depths of his heart and with the uttermost effort of his will, totally and unconditionally surrender.

References

1   Knight, Vol. H, p. 69
2   Knight, Vol. H, p. 69
3   R. H. Benson, *The Friendship of Christ*, Longmans, p. 23
4   R. H. Benson, p. 24
5   R. H. Benson, pp. 26-7
6   R. H. Benson, pp. 29-32

Bubble, Bubble, Toil and Trouble!

TO the uninformed 'man in the street', magic means either conjuring tricks or 'black magic', and enough has been hinted at in the section on the objective Qabalah to reveal that such a thing as ceremonial magic exists and is practised. There is, however, much highly-coloured but unreliable nonsense written about it, and comparatively little that is serious and responsible in intention. This chapter will deal with some aspects of the subject, in so far as they are able to be gleaned from the writing of responsible occultists, informed and experienced in this obscure matter.

W. E. Butler, in his book *The Magician, his Training and Work*, spends some time discussing principles, and then moves on through the techniques of visualization and audition, to discuss the 'magical use of sound' and the use of words and names in magical working. The techniques of vibration are discussed, the colours of the Sephiroth listed, and then comes a discussion of vestments. Of these, Butler says, 'They screen off the personality of the operator, and so make for impersonality. This is of very great importance, especially when magical work is being done by a group comprising both sexes. In some lodges, cowls or hoods are used … The robes have another interesting effect. They act as a very strong autosuggestion, which has the power of keying the mind to the operation in hand. Merely to vest oneself in the robes of one's grade automatically quickens the emotional link which we have with our group or fraternity … From another angle, the robes are of use. During the many magical operations undertaken through the years, the robes become 'charged' with a certain etheric energy.'[1]

The instincts recorded here are not confined altogether to the occult lodges; the Eucharistic vestments have a similar function of covering the personality of the priest and suggesting Christ, whose 'clothes' they are, being stylized replicas of the clothing of the Eastern Roman Empire of the first century. They have a recollecting function too; the act of vesting is a subjective but distinct aid to recollection as any priest knows. Although Christians do not speak of the Eucharistic vestments being 'charged', they are, nevertheless blessed – set apart for this specific purpose. The ceremonial of the Eucharist, the externals, is in a perfectly valid sense 'magical'. It is a subjective, psychological aid, an expression of seemliness. We shall find, in any investigation of ceremonial magic, some familiar ideas, not all of which will provoke disagreement or dismay.

Butler spends some time discussing 'insulation' and the subconscious. Recollection in the form of 'odic armour' is discussed, and a considerable passage is devoted to the 'body of light'.

All inexplicable phenomena are grist to the magician's mill. The frontiers of spiritualism are not inviolate, telepathy, extrasensory perception, levitation, apportation and all kinds of similar, rare but widely experienced and baffling phenomena are sought after and where possible, brought under control. There is a great deal in ceremonial magic which gives the impression of quasi-scientific conjuring. The psychic senses are very deliberately developed, and such faculties as clairvoyance and clairaudience are valued and sought after. It is not difficult to relate all these things to the Tree of Life, for, in spite of their baffling nature, they are manifestly within the natural order and expressions of natural laws not yet fully perceived and understood. After a long period of scepticism, empirical science is at last moving in on a territory peopled hitherto by psychics and magicians. The concept of the collective unconscious, and of the 'within' of things, gives the 'exoteric' something to work with.

One of the exercises Butler is clearly deeply interested in is that of focusing the consciousness *outside* the physical body in what he calls 'the etheric double'. He explains, 'Now the etheric matrix or "double" normally remains in close union with the physical body, and is only separated therefrom and then only partially, by certain drugs, general anaesthetics, mesmerism and hypnotism. When the etheric is driven out of the physical body by any one of these means, a certain amount of it remains with the physical, and between the exteriorized etheric double and the part still remaining on the physical levels, there is what has been termed the "silver cord". Should this cord be broken, then death has occurred.'[2]

In more than one publication Butler has described an astral (or as some occultists would prefer to describe it, an 'etheric') journey 'out of the body'. In the present book, from which we are quoting, he says, 'This is a tremendous experience, and the present writer well remembers the time, now some forty years ago, when, under the guidance of his teacher, he first stood forth in the body of light, and gazed on his earthly form lying in deep trance on the couch. Whoever has this experience *knows* in a mode of absolute knowledge, that he is not the physical body with which he has for so long identified himself.'[3] Butler's description of this experience, in another publication, is very interesting and not unrelated to both psychedelic experience, as recorded by LSD-takers, and, let us be fair, such undoubtedly *religious* experiences as the 'timeless moment', several instances of which have been recorded in Warner Allen's book of that name, by William James in his book, *The Varieties of Religious Experience*, and by F. C. Happold in his book *Mysticism*. It is not possible to pass judgement on another man's experience, but it is worth reminding ourselves of the difference between the objective reality and the subjective response of the senses, in these experiences. The drug-cultist claims religious experience, the occultist claims (certainly seeks) religious experience. The Christian, at his prayers, may have religious experience, but if he is wise he will pay small heed to the *experience* as such as an incidental, reassuring, but essentially unimportant phenomenon. God not experience, is his goal.

The actual technique of projection is outlined in some detail, and we shall not follow this particular matter any further here. The reader may make of it what he will. The perennially awkward question remains: 'So what?'

The construction and use of forms is the title, and the subject matter of one of the chapters in Butler's book, in the section 'Magical Rites'. He writes, 'The principle thought-forms built up in a magical lodge are "the Astral Temple" and the "Godforms", and these are built up most carefully according to a well-established system. In an old-established lodge, there will always be some of the "senior brethren" who are expert in form-construction ... the telesmatic images, as they are termed, are built up by the seniors, but the "temple-form" is built up by all, each member working according to his knowledge and grade." The 'temple-form' is appropriate to the Sephirah being studied. The 'banishing ritual' already described at the beginning of an earlier chapter, includes a circumambulation around the lodge-room, which 'has the effect of building up, in the astral temple, of what appears to clairvoyant vision to be a shimmering wall or barrier of swiftly-moving light. This seems to surround the whole of the lodge, and takes the shape of a half-sphere, whose highest point is directly over the altar; which, in the rituals, is placed in the centre of the lodge floor. Presumably the psychic wall is a full sphere, the other half being under the lodge floor.'[5]

This seems to be, in idea at least, a kind of corporate extension of the 'odic armour' – a corporate recollection, a defence against assault along the unconscious. This idea of assault, of psychic attack, is worth pondering. Those who have had to do with primitive tribes do not need telling that witchcraft works! The Australian aborigine's 'pointing-bone' is a kind of outward sign of a deliberate assault via the unconscious. The primitive man is defenceless, and is killed by mere suggestion.

The purging of the collective unconscious is part of the redemptive work of Christ; not merely in the days of his flesh in the person of Jesus, but throughout the ages in his mystical body, the Church. The prince of this world whom Christ cast out must be perpetually cast out in the power and authority of the Christ. He is defeated by the Holy Name. This is not 'ecclesiastical magic', it is a fact to which the Church must bear witness. *The realm of the demonic is the collective unconscious.* Of this there is no doubt whatever, and it is a grave reproach to the Church that she has too often allowed herself to be 'demythologized' or 'modernized' – in other words blinded – as to the *depths* of her mission. There are not wanting among the clergy even huge numbers who will roar with laughter at the very idea of the demonic in 'these days!' The attitude, 'I have not experienced this, therefore it is not!' is not a good expression of either the humility of Christ, or an understanding of the depths of his mission.

The realm of the demonic is the collective unconscious – the 'within' of things. The 'white magician' seeks to preserve himself from harm by stronger magic. The only 'stronger man' than the devil (however that principle be understood) is he who 'overthrew him and spoiled his goods'. The great peril of exploring the unconscious is that the explorer cannot know what may be riding on his shoulder – or when! Here is the peril of both occultism as a *science* as well as a pseudo-religion, and also of certain forms of psychotherapy. In the confused minds of men, 'religion' and 'science' have seemed, until recently, to be at war. In fact the two disciplines are complementary. Christ is the light by which the scientist must work, and – acknowledged or not – the Holy Spirit is his inspiration!

Without doubt the ceremonial magician can perform many 'tricks' in depth and some, such as Crowley, have claimed to have 'called up' demonic principles and clothed them in forms. The occultist is insistent that carelessness or malice can release such entities, and the Church's power of exorcism is frequently exercised to deal with such troubles. It is an unhappy and unhealthy fact, however, that many so-called 'modern' Christians affect amused disbelief in that with which our Lord was at war throughout his Incarnate Life simply because, 'it has not happened to me!'

The man who taught the novelist Dennis Wheatley all he knew about magic, Mr Rollo Ahmed, has this to say about 'elementals'. 'Elementals are the most elusive forms of spirit beings of which we have knowledge, and can be roughly divided into three categories. First, there are the strange, quasi-intelligent thought-creations, usually of an evil and malevolent character, that dwell upon the lower regions of the astral plane. Secondly there are the so-called Nature Spirits. Thirdly, there are the "shells" or astral simulacra of those whose actual spirits have become sunk in evil to the extinction of the ego. We will turn our attention to the first group … just as man materializes his thoughts in the objective world … so do his unexpressed thoughts create upon the mental plane. Creations of extreme beauty result from harmonious mind-vibrations, but evil and destructive thoughts produce ugly and revolting forms as malevolent and harmful as any "demon" could be.'[6]

Ahmed explains that, in the occult view, these secondary 'creations' are kept in being by the continuation of the thoughts that create them and tend, in the case of the malevolent, to obsess their creators. His explanation for the almost observable degeneration of the chronically selfish into a self-destroying paranoia is thus easily guessed. After discussing various manifestations, he continues, 'The elemental is one of the types of spirits especially attracted by acts of sorcery, and contacted by means of human sacrifice and bloodshed. In appearance these creatures vary very greatly. Sometimes they are semi-human, or half-animal, and again may have a completely grotesque aspect or a huge slug-like form. They frequently seem shapeless and indefinite in outline, and their presence can be detected by a terrible smell that is sometimes noticeable even to the material sense. … Thought forms can be deliberately built up in any aspect we choose, and sent out to do our bidding. This power can be used for good; but the black magician employs it to injure, destroy and cause bitterness, hatred, strife and immorality. He clothes such forms in the shape he desires to influence people in accordance with his own will, and for whatever end and purpose he desires. But in this form of black magic, as in all others, there is a price to pay, and the time comes when the sorcerer has to deal with the creatures he has created, and only too often they turn upon him to his destruction.'[7]

Mumbo-jumbo, a rather purposeless flexing of the esoteric muscles, and a ghastly danger inherent in all 'dabblings', might seem to many to be the sum total of ceremonial magic. This might be a natural enough reaction, but it is not quite fair. Let us, by way of conclusion, hear Israel Regardie on the use of ceremonial magic to good intent. Writing of the techniques of evoking into visible appearance in 'the magical triangle of manifestation', he asks, 'What is the technical process of rendering objective these autonomous partial systems?' He is referring to psychoneuroses. 'Magic parts company here with orthodox psychology ... the magical theory prefers a drastic form of emotional and mental excitation by means of a ceremonial technique. During the evocation ceremony, divine and spirit names are continuously vibrated as part of a lengthy conjuration. Circumambulations are performed from symbolic positions in the temple ... by means of these exercises, consciousness is stimulated to such a degree as to become opened, despite itself, to the enforced updwelling of the content of the unconscious ... the particular partial-system is then exuded from the sphere of sensation and projected outwards. It embodies itself in so-called astral or etheric substance normally comprising the interior body which serves as the foundation or design of the physical form, and acting as the bridge between the body and the mind, of which it is the vehicle. The astral form now reflecting the partial system projected from the unconscious, attracts to itself particles of heavy incense burned copiously during the ceremony. Gradually, in the course of the ceremonial, a materialization is built up which has the shape and character of an autonomous being. It can be spoken to and it can speak. Likewise it can be directed and controlled by the operator of the ceremony. At the conclusion of the operation, it is absorbed deliberately and consciously back into the operator by the usual formula. "And now I say unto thee, depart from hence with the blessing of – (the appropriate divine name governing that particular type of complex) – upon thee. And let there ever be peace between me and thee. And be thou ever ready to come and obey my will, whether it be by a ceremony or but by a gesture."[8]

This is an exercise in 'magical psycho-analysis', and let us close this chapter with the final word on the subject that Regardie has to say; it is thought-provoking! 'I hope one day to see a modification of it (this technique) in current use by our psychologists.'[9]

References

1   W. E. Butler, *The Magician, His Training and Work*, pp. 86-7
2   W. E. Butler, p. 115
3   W. E. Butler, p. 116
4   W. E. Butler, pp. 131-2
5   W. E. Butler, p. 134
6   Rollo Ahmed, *The Black Art*, John Long Ltd, p. 244
7   Rollo Ahmed, pp. 246-9
8   Israel Regardie, *The Art and Meaning of Magic*, Helios, pp. 56-7
9   Israel Regardie, p. 58

Stimulating the Primitive

'ONE of the most interesting and important points in occultism is that of psychic and occult contacts. That is, if occult work is to be anything more than a feeble "pussy-cat occultism".' So writes W. E. Butler. 'Far too much of modern occultism consists of such feeble work in the realms of force that it is quite possibly true that the Dark Masters are content to let such efforts pass unheeded, as being unworthy of their powder and shot. Such a state of affairs clearly indicates one thing at least, that such societies and organizations are not deeply rooted and are not properly contacted upon the inner planes.'[1] This statement will serve to lead us to examine one of the great interests of the occultist, the stimulation of his latent psychic sense, more usually known to him as clairvoyance.

This book has been concerned with theory and theology to a much greater degree than a typical occultist would find necessary. Christians realize that right belief is vital and conditions everything. The occultist is practical and pragmatic; he is concerned with experience and results. 'Does it work?' 'What happens?' These are his first questions; his theology, such as it is, is arrived at subjectively with much borrowing and many inconsistencies, none of which really worry him. It is his experience which leads him to construct working hypotheses and it is thus small wonder that they are pantheistic and also Gnostic in character.

The psychic sense, operating through the unconscious, both collective and individual, brings the contents of the unconscious into conscious awareness, though not a really objective awareness. It is sub-rational and a relic of man's past, but it is nevertheless the source of a very great deal of the occultist's experience *and it is this that he would describe as mystical.* The novelist Dennis Wheatley, an authority on occultism (but as an outsider, as he is quick to point out), refers to occultists on more than one occasion in his works as 'mystics'. When this term is used, it is the exercise of clairvoyance, with the aid of such stimulants as astrology and other forms of divination, that is the 'mysticism' in question. This is the occultist's understanding of the word, to a large extent, but the Christian would not for a moment associate 'mysticism' with such exercises. The editor of a recently published symposium of occult writings complains of the danger of esoteric symbolism and practical method being lost to posterity, due partly 'to efforts of its custodians of this century to substitute a mild form of Christian mysticism for the traditional magical and psychic techniques'.[2] It is very hard for the Christian to imagine what the writer means by 'a mild form of Christian mysticism'. The expression is an astonishing contradiction in terms! When it is realized that 'mysticism' has a totally different meaning to the occultist, and that 'Christian' in this context might mean literally anything, then the Christian will be as eager as the occultist to deprecate it!

The psychic principle is something sadly neglected by the Church as a whole. There are reasons for this and not all of them are bad reasons, but it will be seen that the Christian would place severe restrictions on its stimulation and use, as we shall see.

The whole process of evolution, not merely of man but of creation as a whole, appears to have been the evolution and emergence of *consciousness*. This we have already stated in an earlier chapter. The process attains its highest point in man in whom consciousness acquires a wholly new dimension, that of reflection and rationality. The rational principle itself is in process of constant refinement, and whereas in former millennia communication between men was largely psychic, via the unconscious (as in the case of the higher animals), to a greater and greater extent man has learned to communicate via his reflective consciousness in rational thought and the spoken word. As the evolution of man continues in Christ, the psychic becomes redundant and gives place to the rational; magic gives place to science. The psychic faculty, no longer necessary to modern man, begins to fade until great numbers of people are found in whom it seems to be wholly absent, and greater numbers still in whom it is quite dormant (save perhaps for a brief 'flutter' at puberty). Many perceptive souls would deny the very existence of the faculty on the grounds that it savours of superstition and they have no personal awareness of any such sense themselves. This is an arrogant position and in many it is merely a defence mechanism, but they are at least preserved from the temptation – the very dangerous temptation – to 'dabble'. In one thing such people are right; the psychic faculty is indeed closely connected with superstition and darkness for it is the faculty which not only brings the contents of the unconscious up into sub-rational awareness, it is also the faculty which encounters the demonic whose realm is, as we have seen, the collective unconscious in the wider understanding of that term. We can repeat our conviction here that the collective unconscious is the realm of the prince of this world – that is what the title means! The Incarnate Lord, being the stronger, overthrew him.

The Christian is simply not interested in being psychic. This is totally irrelevant to his Christian profession and is of no more consequence than the colour of his hair. In Christ, the whole direction of his gaze has been changed; his relationship with his Lord is one of integration, ever more fully realized, based upon mutual self-giving love. The Christian life consists in the free conformity of the human will to that of God, aided by grace. In Christ the Christian learns to look through the eyes of Christ and see only God. He no longer seeks fulfilment within the depths of Creation; rather, he seeks fulfilment *for* creation, and his gaze in fact *transcends creation*.

If it be the will of God for him that Christ shall operate in his world through one of the human faculties, then that faculty will be awakened and developed. This is occasionally true of those who are naturally psychic because the overthrow of the prince of this world is an eternal operation, performed by the Incarnate Lord in time and continued by him throughout time in his body, the Church. Through the members of his body, the Church, the Christ exorcises evil. Further than this, the liberation of souls who are unquiet is an eternal exercise to be performed throughout time. The Crucified Lord preached to the spirits in prison, and this he still does through the members of his mystical body in whom he has awakened the psychic faculty as a channel of grace, bringing love, peace and absolution to souls in need of it. There are not a few devout Christians, near to our Lord, whose awakened psychic faculty enables them to bear the burdens of the unquiet and communicate the love of Christ to them. As we have already observed, the failure of so many Christians, who really should know better, to acknowledge the depths of Christ's ministry, is a matter of sorrow and reproach.

To the Christian, therefore, the psychic faculty is a thing of no great consequence in itself; a relic of man's sub-rational past and a memory of his former thraldom. Activated by God as an instrument of grace, it is to be used with the uttermost care and with the profoundest recollection, and then only in those instances when God provides an occasion for its use as an Instrument of grace.

The occultist, unable to transcend creation, is forced to rely upon the psychic faculty to provide him with much of the experience of what seems to him to represent reality. He too is sensitive to the dangers from the demonic, but deprived of the transcendent victory of Christ, he must trust to his own right intentions (as he conceives them) and stronger magic, to fight off the powder and shot of the 'dark masters'. The dangers to which he is subjected are extreme. He seeks to know, to have powers, in order to serve; but to serve whom? 'My fellow men' he will answer, and he may very well mean it. But alas, there is a tremendous difference between 'doing good' and the self-abnegation that results in the Christ serving the images of God in God's world through the members of his mystical body. No judgement is intended upon a man's desire to serve but it is possible to 'do good' in arrogance, not as 'he who serveth' but as 'he who manipulateth, or pusheth around'. The confirmed 'dogooder' has, all too often, a love of Power and a boundless self-esteem. The occultist, be he never so sincere, is faced with grave dangers not all of which he can hope to be aware of. He must ever present a hunted appearance for all the Power he seeks – or claims – to command.

Modern occultism exhibits a number of interesting trends, none more so than the separation out of a determinedly controlled and rational exercise from a sub-rational, essentially psychic one. As yet, the terms are used loosely and distinctions are by no means hard-and-fast, but the two types of 'projection', astral and etheric, are a case in point.

Astral projection, as understood by the school of thought represented by Gareth Knight, is a development of the imaginative symbol-projection that we have already studied in which such a high degree of concentration and involvement is sought that all contact is lost with the 'earthly vehicle'. Not every occultist would see the necessity for going to such lengths, and not all could attempt it (let alone succeed). The end result would seem to be a kind of trance state (but trance is very difficult to define), or perhaps a very intense exercise like that of 'rising on the planes' (a Western equivalent of Kundalini Yoga) or even the forming of an imagined simulacrum of the self and the deliberate transfer of consciousness into it, such as we studied in an earlier chapter. This latter exercise, however, has more in common with the second type of projection, also called 'astral' by many occultists, but 'etheric' by Knight and others.

Etheric projection is a technique essentially psychic in character which, although it may sound fantastic to many people, is nevertheless by no means unknown. There are known to the present writer those who, with little effort, can 'visit' the old folks at home and see how they are getting on without ever getting up out of their office chair. This ability has to be kept severely in check because its use amounts to a use of Power for personal ends, however innocent those ends may be. The strict morality of the use of psychic gifts is an ever-taxing question to those so gifted, and they are wise to err on the side of rigourism. The writer also knows of the 'discovery' at long range, by a Malayan village 'pawang' of a soldier, lost in thick jungle; also of the body of a murder victim buried in a flooded paddy field. Another friend of the writer was assured by a member of her family whom she described as 'most odd' of the safety of relatives after the fall of

Singapore. The 'most odd' relative was an occultist, one of the authorities quoted in this book, who used power magically for a benevolent end. The use of the psychic faculty in water divining is an instance in which the morality of its use is hardly an issue, but as a general rule, the moral issue is very much a live one. A hairsbreadth distinguishes between the paths which lead a man to become a man of God on one hand, and a man of power on the other. The distinction is absolute, however, and eternal.

The magical-cum-religious system of the Celts established lines of psychic communication, traceable to this day on the map as a system of triangles and pentangles. It has been the experience of not a few psychic people to find themselves, when on a 'line', either knowingly or unknowingly, suddenly and inexplicably aware of what is going on at the other end of the line. The points of intersection and the apices of the triangles are normally the sites on which the cult was practised and they are frequently places where a considerable disturbance can be made, psychically, by unwise 'dabbling'. Those who tinker with the occult have no idea, as a rule, what they are doing and the 'noise' they are making. Nor do they realize the dangers to their souls and their sanity.

Dennis Wheatley, in his novel, *Strange Conflict*, makes astral or etheric projection the main feature of the work. Much of what he writes as fiction is within the experience of certain psychic people as fact, but naturally enough, the storyteller's licence is very considerable and the psychic faculty is stretched well beyond its capacity, a fact for which we should probably be thankful. The book is a clear and lucid statement of much occult belief; Karma and reincarnation, the many-tiered universe, and the doctrine of the inevitable triumph of good over evil is well stated; magical operations are clearly described and it is an excellent story based on a good deal of scholarship in these matters. The projection of consciousness is a matter of experience, the phenomenon of levitation is widely authenticated and that of apportation is by no means unknown. Of this latter phenomenon, the Theosophist 'Bishop' Leadbeater wrote that the removal of a glass of water from England to Australia by esoteric means was perfectly possible, but the effort involved would be out of all proportion to the end in view. The apportation, by magicians, of drugs to addicts may sound like something out of Mr Wheatley's more colourful novels, but it is a phenomenon capable of being vouched for.

The distinction between astral projection and etheric possibly represents the separation out of an intentionally rational exercise from an essentially sub-rational one. Certainly, the correspondence between esoteric mediation and psychotherapeutic techniques indicates an emergence of 'science' from magic in the best traditions; those which distilled chemistry from alchemy and astrophysics from astrology. The separation out is not yet very far advanced, however, and it is still possible for a very closely and carefully prepared meditation sequence according to Celtic mythology to be advanced as the key to 'the power to function as a member of the priesthood of the *old religion*'.[3]

The Christian, once again, finds himself asking the question, 'so what?' These psychic exercises are pointless in themselves; the saints in whom they were manifest are insistent that they are to be avoided where possible and ignored if they cannot be avoided. Psychic phenomena have, of themselves, no significance whatever, but the uses to which they can be put are of very great moral consequence. Phenomena and faculties of this kind are not to be desired or sought after, they are rather to be endured and subjected at all times to the will of God. The Christian knows that the psychic, when it manifests, must be subjected to, and give place to the rational. The Christian seeks God as he is in himself, not his gifts nor the 'experiences' of 'religion'. It is right that the Christian should seek, by the inspiration of the Holy Spirit, the key to the workings of the universe, the conquest of the air, the mechanics of the mind – and union with God himself. It is much less likely to be right that he should seek, by stimulation of the primitive psychic faculty, to be a 'flying soul' and be able to call upon Power. The two quests do not go in the same direction.

The right intentions of the sane occultist are summed up very well in *Strange Conflict*, in which Dennis Wheatley's hero, the Duke, engaged in a conflict with a Satanist in the context of the Second World War, suddenly 'sees the light'.

'He had always known that in his magical operations he was not quite White, but just a little Grey. He had not used his powers for self-advancement or personal aims, but almost unwittingly he still allowed his own deep-rooted passions and convictions to influence him. For example, he did not regard the Nazis from an entirely detached point of view, as a menace to the welfare of mankind; he *hated* them, with all the hatred with which his virile personality was capable; and that was wrong. Perhaps it was because of that slight uncertainty of his own powers that in his magical operations he had always followed the rituals of the text-books and utilized such things as garlic, asafoetida grass, crucifixes, horseshoes and many other symbols. These things in themselves were, he knew, only focuses to attract power; they had not an atom of power in themselves, but were just bundles of herbs or pieces of wood and iron. A pure white magician, confident in his own strength, would have despised them and relied entirely upon his own will. Without any of these things, or pentacles, or mumbled phrases from ancient mysteries, he would have gone out, fearless and alone from his body on to the astral to give battle. In that strange moment all things were made clear to the Duke. He had been a coward. He had shirked the conflict when he should have gone out to fight, relying alone upon the intrinsic fact that Light is more powerful than darkness.'[4]

The Christian's reply is given in another novel, *That Hideous Strength* by C. S. Lewis, in which Merlin, awakened from his great sleep, seeks to heal a friend's wounds by his old arts.

'The room was heavy with a sort of floating anaesthesia. "Through me," said Merlin, "you can suck up from the Earth oblivion of all pains." "Silence," said the Director sharply. The magician started and straightened himself. ... "No," said the Director. " God's glory, do you think you were dug out of the earth to give me a plaster for my heel? We have drugs that could cheat the pain as well as your magic, if it were not my business to bear it to the end. I will hear no more of that." "I hear and obey," said the magician. "But I meant no harm. If not to heal your wound, yet for the healing of Logres, you will need my commerce with field and water." Again that sweet heaviness, like the smell of hawthorn. "No," said the Director, "that cannot be done any longer. The soul has gone out of the wood and water. Oh, I dare say you could awaken them – a little. But it would not be enough. Your weapon would break in your hands. For the hideous strength confronts us, and it is as in the days when Nimrod built a tower to reach heaven." "Hidden it may be," said Merlinus, "but not *changed*. Leave me to work, Lord. I will wake it." "No," said the Director, "I forbid it. Whatever of spirit may still linger in the earth has withdrawn fifteen hundred years farther away from us since your time. You shall not lift your little finger to call it up. It is in this age utterly unlawful." He leaned forward and said in a different voice, "It never was very lawful, even in your day."'[5]

References

1   W. E. Butler in *New Dimmsions Red Book*, ed. Wilby, p. 5
2   *Red Book* editorial
3   F. P. D. in *Red Book*, p. 88
4   Dennis Wheatley, *Strange Conflict*, p. 262
5   C. S. Lewis, *That Hideous Strength*, p. 176

Not a Conclusion

AT the beginning of this book, in the preface, the desire was expressed to keep this book, as far as possible, 'open ended'. By the very nature of the subject matter, no conclusions are possible to the Christian; he stands where he stands, and views with all the charity and appreciation he can command a pre-Christian speculative system of great complexity, and yet one of astonishing unity. He will call to mind the rise of the great science of astronomy out of the mumbo-jumbo, the insights, the speculations and the observations of astrology. He will remember that chemistry owes its origins to a similar hotchpotch of profundity and moonshine known as alchemy. All along the line, magic and esotericism give place to – give birth to – empirical sciences to the great benefit of man and the glory of God. Now, in the stream of occultism we have briefly – and let it be remembered – superficially studied, we see – alongside and within – the beginnings of psychology and many of the techniques of psychotherapy. There is more to come. The phenomena which man grudgingly acknowledges but cannot fit into his current understanding of things will, in due time, yield their secrets. The occult will ever give place to the empirical because occultism at its best *is* empirical.

What else will come to mind as the Christian turns this all over in his consciousness? After the revulsions, the griefs, the sadnesses – and the laughs too – what thoughts will emerge?

One of them may be this: that Christ, the great secularizer, will begin to liberate this intricate structure from the cloying and fundamentally irrelevant clutches of – 'religion'. In so doing, its true nature will begin to emerge more clearly and its inherent merits and demerits will be the better perceived.

In an earlier chapter, we asked ourselves why the Christian feels able to approach the same basic technique in two distinct minds? Why does he feel interested and open-minded about the psychotherapists use of magical techniques, while he is disturbed and repelled by the occultist's use of the self-same techniques? The key to this is the word 'religion'. The one use was relevant to its purpose; the other irrelevant and misguided. The Christian will, if he is wise, regard the occultist with great compassion. He will pray that the occultist's researches may pass into the light of Christ which illuminates science. He will pray too that the occultist, liberated from 'religion' may be brought to reality and grow into the measure of the stature of the fulness of Christ.

Appendix A to Part Three

The twenty-two paths between the ten Sephiroth represent the 'Subjective Qabalah' and have their own Yetziratic Texts, colours and symbols. The second volume of Gareth Knight's work, *A Practical Guide to Qabalistic Symbolism*, deals with the paths in great detail, and from this the following table of symbols is compiled. It is incomplete, but for a fuller treatment the reader is referred to Knight's work.

Path	Tarot Trump Card	Hebrew Letter	Astrological Sign	Theory	Colours
11	The Fool	Aleph	Air	Spirit of Aether	Bright pale yellow, sky blue, blue, emerald, emerald flecked gold
12	The Magus	Beth	Mercury	Magus of Power	Yellow, purple, grey, indigo flecked violet
13	The High Priestess	Gimel	Moon	Priestess of the Silver Star	Blue, silver, cold pale blue, silver rayed sky blue
14	The Empress	Daleth	Venus	Daughter of the Mighty Ones	Emerald green, sky blue, early spring green, bright rose, cerise rayed pale green
15	The Star	Heh	Aries	Daughter of the Firmament, Dweller between the Waters	Scarlet, red, brilliant flame, glowing red
16	The Hierophant	Vau	Taurus	Magus of the Eternal	Red orange, deep indigo, deep warm olive, rich brown
17	The Lovers	Zain	Gemini	Children of the Voice, Oracle of the Mighty Gods	Orange, pale mauve, new yellow leather, reddish grey inclined to mauve
18	The Chariot	Cheth	Cancer	Child of the Powers of the Waters, Lord of the Triumph of Light	Amber, maroon, rich bright russet, dark greenish brown
19	Strength	Teth	Leo	Daughter of the Flaming Sword, Leader of the Lion	Greenish yellow, deep purple, grey, reddish yellow
20	The Hermit	Yod	Virgo	Prophet of the Eternal, Magus of the Voice of Power	Yellowish green, slate grey, green-grey, plum

Path	Tarot Trump Card	Hebrew Letter	Astrological Sign	Theory	Colours
21	The Wheel of Fortune	Kaph	Jupiter	Lord of the Forces of Life	Violet, blue, rich purple, bright blue rayed yellow
22	Justice	Lamed	Libra	Daughter of the Lords of Truth, Ruler of the Balance	Emerald, blue, deep blue-green, pale green
23	The Hanged Man	Mem	Water	Spirit of the Mighty Waters	Deep blue, sea green, deep olive green, white flecked purple
24	Death	Nun	Scorpio	Child of the Great Transformers, Lord of the Gates of Death	Green-blue, dull brown, very dark brown, livid indigo brown
25	Temperance	Samekh	Sagittarius	Daughter of the Reconcilers, Bringer Forth of Life	Blue, yellow, green, dark vivid blue
26	The Devil	Ayin	Capricorn	Lord of the Gates of Matter, Child of the Forces of Time	Indigo, black, blue-black, cold very dark grey
27	The Tower (The House of God)	Peh	Mars	Lord of the Hosts of the Mighty	Scarlet, red, venetian red, bright red rayed azure and emerald
28	The Emperor	Tzaddi	Aquarius	Son of the Morning Chief among the Mighty	Violet, sky-blue, bluish-mauve, white tinged purple
29	The Moon	Qoph	Pisces	Ruler of Flux and Reflux, Child of the Sons of the Mighty	Crimson, buff flecked silver-white, light translucent pinkish-brown, stone
30	The Sun	Resh	Sun	Lord of the Fire of the World	Orange, gold yellow, rich amber, amber rayed red
31	The Last Judgement	Shin	Fire	Spirit of the Primal Fire	Glowing orange scarlet, vermilion, scarlet flecked gold, vermilion flecked crimson and emerald
32	The Universe	Tau	Saturn	Great One of the Night of Time	Indigo, blue-black, black rayed blue

NB: The attribution of tarot trumps to the various paths varies to some extent between traditions within occultism, as does the design of the tarot cards themselves.

Appendix B to Part Three

Beginning his chapter on the tarot court cards, Gareth Knight says: 'The court cards of the tarot are sixteen in number – four to each suit and some confusion has arisen over their exact nomenclature. In the modern playing cards there are three court cards only to each suit – king, queen, knave or jack. In the tarot there is additionally a figure on horseback and this has been generally called the knight. A tradition has thus grown up to call the seated tarot court figures the king and queen; the equestrian figure the knight; and the standing figure the page or princess. This is not altogether a happy arrangement as it obscures the symbolic issues.'[1]

Knight examines these symbolic issues at some length and gives us the esoteric titles of the tarot court cards, which are as follows:

Wands   Ace – Root of the Powers of Fire
        Knight – Lord of Flame and Lightning, King of the Spirits of Fire
        Queen – Queen of the Thrones of Flame
        King – Prince of the Chariot of Fire
        Knave – Princess of the Shining Flame, Rose of the Palace of Fire

Cups   Ace – Root of the Powers of Water
        Knight – Lord of the Waves and the Waters, King of the Hosts of the Sea
        Queen – Queen of the Thrones of the Waters
        King – Prince of the Chariot of the Waters
        Knave – Princess of the Waters and the Lotus

Swords   Ace – Root of the Powers of Air
        Knight – Lord of the Wind and the Breezes, Lord of the Spirits of the Air
        Queen – Queen of the Thrones of the Air
        King – Prince of the Chariot of the Wind
        Knave – Princess of the Rushing Winds, Lotus of the Palace of Air

Disks*   Ace – Root of the Powers of Earth
        Knight – Lord of the Wide and Fertile Land, King of the Spirits of Earth
        Queen – Queen of the Thrones of Earth
        King – Prince of the Chariot of Earth
        Knave – Princess of the Echoing Hills, Rose of the Palace of Earth[2]

* Dion Fortune refers to this suit as pentacles

1   Gareth Knight, *A Practical Guide to Qabalistic Symbolism*, Vol. II, p. 255
2   Gareth Knight, *A Practical Guide to Qabalistic Symbolism*, Vol. II, pp. 258-9

Appendix C to Part Three

A Short Bibliography of Occult Writings

Gareth Knight,   *A Practical Guide to Qabalistic Symbolism*, Helios, 1965

Dion Fortune,   *The Mystical Qabalah*, Benn, 1935 (seventh impression 1966)
                Applied Magic
                Psychic Self-Defence
                Practical Occultism in Daily Life
                The Cosmic Doctrine
                Aspects of Occultism
                Esoteric Philosophy of Love and Marriage
                Esoteric Orders and their Work
                The Training and Work of an Initiate
                Sane Occultism
                Spiritualism in the Light of Occult Science
                Through the Gates of Death
                (Also a number of occult novels, and a number of works on
                mysticism, psychology, etc., under the name of Violet M. Firth)

Israel Regardie,   *The Art of True Healing*, Helios, 1964
                The Art and Meaning of Magic, Helios, 1964
                A Garden of Pomegranates
                The Tree of Life
                My Rosicrucian Adventure
                The Middle Pillar
                The Philosophers' Stone
                The Golden Dawn (4 vols., published 1940)
                The Romance of Metaphysics
                Magic and the Qabalah, Aquarian

W. E. Butler,   *The Magician, His Training and Work*, Aquarian, 1963
                Magic: Its Ritual, Power and Purpose, Aquarian
                Apprenticed to Magic, Aquarian

Eliphas Levi,   *The History of Magic*, tr. A. E. Waite,
                Transcendental Magic, Rider

Wynn Westcott,   *Sepher Yetzirah*

S. L. Macgregor   *The Qabalah Unveiled*
Mathers,

Aleister Crowley,   *Magick in Theory and Practice*, Castle

Rollo Ahmed,   *The Black Art*, Long, 1936

Helios Book   *The New Dimensions Red Book*, ed. Wilby
Service Ltd.,   *Helios Course on the Practical Qabalah*

Index

CPSIA information can be obtained
at www.ICGtesting.com
Printed in the USA
BVHW080641080121
597260BV00006B/451